Opening
the Door
to Your
God-Sized
Dream

Books by Holley Gerth

You're Already Amazing
The "Do What You Can" Plan (ebook)
You're Made for a God-Sized Dream

Opening the Door
to Your
God-Sized
Dream

40 Days of Encouragement for Your Heart

Holley Gerth

Revell

a division of Baker Publishing Group
Grand Rapids, Michigan

© 2013 by Holley Gerth

Published by Revell
a division of Baker Publishing Group
P.O. Box 6287, Grand Rapids, MI 49516-6287
www.revellbooks.com

Printed in the United States of America

Library of Congress Cataloging-in-Publication Data is on file at the Library of Congress, Washington, DC.

ISBN 978-0-8007-2280-7

Unless otherwise indicated, all Scripture quotations are from the Holy Bible, New International Version®. NIV®. Copyright © 1973, 1978, 1984, 2011 by Biblica, Inc.™ Used by permission of Zondervan. All rights reserved worldwide. www.zondervan.com

Scripture quotations identified KJV are from the King James Version of the Bible.

Scripture quotations identified NASB are from the New American Standard Bible®, copyright © 1960, 1962, 1963, 1968, 1971, 1972, 1973, 1975, 1977, 1995 by The Lockman Foundation. Used by permission.

Scripture quotations identified NKJV are from the New King James Version. Copyright © 1982 by Thomas Nelson, Inc. Used by permission. All rights reserved.

Scripture quotations identified NRSV are from the New Revised Standard Version of the Bible, © 1989, by the Division of Christian Education of the National Council of the Churches of Christ in the United States of America. Used by permission. All rights reserved.

In keeping with biblical principles of creation stewardship, Baker Publishing Group advocates the responsible use of our natural resources. As a member of the Green Press Initiative, our company uses recycled paper when possible. The text paper of this book is composed in part of post-consumer waste.

13   14   15   16   17   18   19   7   6   5   4   3   2   1

To the

God-Sized Dreams Team

Contents

Introduction

God-sized dream = *a desire in your heart for more of what God has for you*

The coffee steams up from my cup. The chatter of other conversations swirls around me. The baristas are busy at their work.

I'm here to write about God-sized dreams. And a voice within me keeps insisting, "It's not the right time."

"You're too busy."

"It's too hard."

I know that voice. It comes whenever I get ready to take the next step toward what God has for me. Maybe you've heard it too?

"When you have more experience . . ."

"When the kids are older . . ."

"When the bank account is fuller . . ."

But here's the thing: there is no perfect time for a God-sized dream.

God-sized dreams knock on the door of our hearts. We can get so used to the sound that we let them stand outside for a lifetime. They don't force their way in, insist to be heard, or demand to be pursued.

We have to choose to let our God-sized dreams into our lives. In the middle of the busy. In the middle of the insecurity. In the middle of the fear.

When you open the door of your heart to a God-sized dream, you also open it wider to the Giver of them. That's what matters most of all. If you long for more intimacy with Jesus, joy in your life, purpose in your days, then put your hand on the doorknob and get ready to turn it.

Will it be a little scary? Yes.

Will it probably be harder than you thought? Yes.

Will it be more worth it than you could have even imagined? Absolutely.

Close your eyes for a moment. Listen not with your ears but with the deepest part of you.

Tap-tap.

It's there.

A God-sized dream waiting not for the perfect time but for this one—*waiting for this moment*. Right here. Right now.

Let's open the door together.

I'll be right there with you as you do.

And best of all, God will too.

1

Giving Words to Your God-Sized Dream

In the beginning was the Word . . .

John 1:1

The question comes quietly, "Have you ever shared your God-sized dream with anyone?"

It's posted online in a group of ninety-nine God-sized dreamers. You can almost hear the nervous laughter spread throughout the thread.

A few answers appear: Yes, I've shared my God-sized dream with . . .

My husband.

My best friend.

Someone at my church.

But more common than those answers are the confessions that putting words to a God-sized dream is downright scary.

What if it doesn't come true?

What if I fail?

What if this isn't what God has for me after all?

I nod my head in understanding at these questions. It's one thing to have a quiet desire within your heart. It's quite another to let it have a voice.

And yet all the way back to the start of creation, God shows us words have incredible power. The story of earth opens with creation being spoken into being.

Let there be light.

Let the land produce.

Let us make mankind in our image.

Opening the Door to Your God-Sized Dream

Let is a word of permission. It's an opening up, an inviting in, a bringing forth. What is the "let there be . . ." that needs to be spoken in your life?

When God says, "Let there be . . ." the same response always follows: "And there was." For the Creator of the universe, words and results always align. For us finite humans, the process unfolds differently.

First, it takes time for our God-sized dreams to fully come into being. We can get discouraged when the vision doesn't instantly become reality. But only God has that capability. God-sized dreams take perseverance.

Also, what God envisions and what happens are one and the same because he has perfect perspective. For us, our God-sized dreams usually turn out very differently than we imagined when we began. They require flexibility as we let our original plan be reshaped to God's will.

And for our dreams to become reality, our words have to be followed with action. Once we put words to our dreams, it's easy to think that's all it takes. But that's only the beginning. Our words become the driver for what we do . . . again and again, day after day.

I glance once more at the responses from the God-sized dream team online. The fear is slowly giving way to excitement, support, and joy. As they share their hearts, I can feel the beat within their words. Like the first blip on an ultrasound when new life appears.

Small but powerful.
Full of promise.
The beginning of good things.

Let there be . . .
a God-sized dream in your life today.

Explore

Read John 1:1–5 to discover more about the Word and his creative work in our lives and hearts.

Express

God, thank you that you are the Creator of all things and all true dreams. It's a little scary to put

Opening the Door to Your God-Sized Dream

words to mine, but at the same time I know doing so brings life and power into what you're asking me to do in mysterious ways. Give me courage to say yes to what you're asking me to do, and most of all, help me to draw closer today to you. Amen.

Experience

You've put your God-sized dream into words. Now try drawing it here. (Disclaimer: I have no artistic skills, and it's okay if you don't either.) Practice going through the process God did at creation—going from what you say to what you can see.

2

What If You Don't Know Your God-Sized Dream?

"What no eye has seen,
what no ear has heard,
and what no human mind has
conceived"—
the things God has prepared for
those who love him—
these are the things God has revealed
to us by his Spirit.

1 Corinthians 2:9–10

As women begin to chatter online about their God-sized dreams, I notice a quieter conversation

20

taking place too. It slips into my inbox through emails, finds its way to the comment sections on my blog, and is even whispered over the phone by friends in my real life. Everywhere I hear this same question: What if I don't know what my God-sized dream is right now? If that's you as you're beginning this journey, then know you're not alone—lots of your sisters are with you.

And even if you're totally clear about your God-sized dream right now, there may be a time when you're not as sure.

So let me lean in and gently whisper to your heart words you need to hear now or that you can tuck away into your heart for later: Don't worry, beautiful friend. You really do have a God-sized dream.

Because all God-sized dreams are ultimately just this: a desire for more of what God has for you. And you want that, don't you? Yep, I thought so.

Some of us have specific ways we want to experience that in our lives, like a particular calling or project. But really at the heart of all of those things is the same ultimate goal . . . *to make life an intimate adventure with God.*

In many ways, God-sized dreaming is more about an attitude than an action. It's living with an ongoing yes to whatever God asks of you.

It means choosing faith over fear.

It means moving forward instead of holding back.

It means believing God can accomplish his purposes for your life—no matter how hard things are right now.

Jesus said the two most important things in life are this: love God, love people (Mark 12:30–31). That's true of every God-sized dream. So if you're not sure what words or goals to put to your dream yet, start there. Simply say, "My dream is to grow in my love for God and people."

That's your heart, isn't it? What you really want? I may not know you, but I believe that's true of you.

As you go through the following weeks, you may get more details about what that means in your life. Or it might stay vague. Either one is okay. You might discover you have one dream that stands out or lots of different ideas. That's okay too.

Where we're going is more about the journey than the destination. Even those of us who think we know where God is leading us are probably going to be surprised where we end up. (Yes, I speak from experience on that one!)

So let's begin together by turning our hearts to God and to whatever he has for us....

A God-Sized Dreamer's Prayer

God, your thoughts are not my thoughts (Isa. 55:8).

What you have planned for me is beyond all I can ask or imagine (Eph. 3:19–20).

Yet you have also promised to reveal it to me through your Spirit (1 Cor. 2:8–10).

So I open my heart, mind, and life to more of you—to whatever you have for me. Where there is ongoing fear in my life, please replace it with faith. Where there is a desire to hold back, give me the strength to move forward. Where there is a desert, lead me into the Promised Land you have prepared for me.

I embrace that my part is to pray, plan, and most of all seek you. And yours is to get me where you want me to go (Prov. 16:9 and 19:21).

What If You Don't Know Your God-Sized Dream?   23

*Wherever that is, that's where I want to be too.
Because there's no better place in this world
or the next than with you (Ps. 84:10).*

*Your kingdom come, your will be done, on
earth (especially my little corner of it) as it is
in heaven (Matt. 6:10).*

In Jesus's name, amen.

So will you take this journey with me, sister?
Even if you don't know exactly where it's leading
in your life?

I can promise you'll be heading to somewhere
good—because that's who God is.

And he's the very best dream of all.

Explore
....

Take time to read the Scriptures from the God-
Sized Dreamer's Prayer above.

Express
....

*God, there is so much I don't know about you and
your plans for my life. But I'm certain of this one*

thing: I want more of you and whatever you have for me. I pray you will lead me forward through your Spirit. I'm excited about going on a new adventure with you! Amen.

Experience

Sometimes our God-sized dreams are closer than we think. Take a few minutes to think back over your life and the desires of your heart—even as a child. What did you really love? What did you feel most excited about? Hidden within your answers may be the seed of a God-sized dream.

3

Say Yes Anyway

Now faith is confidence in what we hope for and assurance about what we do not see.

Hebrews 11:1

As soon as you try to put words to your God-sized dream, more words will come. Words like, "What if . . ." or "What will I do about . . ."

There's a part of us that insists, "You have to get all of those questions resolved before you take a step forward." But if you wait for that, then you will never pursue your God-sized dream.

Because God-sized dreams are about faith.

If you are certain about everything, then it's no longer about trust in the Giver of the dream. And what he wants most on this journey is your heart.

I'm not saying to plunge foolishly ahead. Do your due diligence. Pray, ask for wise counsel, and do practical research. But at some point you have to actually do something.

When you do, it will feel like the world is going to explode. Your heart will try to beat out of your chest. Your mind will swirl like a little tornado. Your knees will knock right there in your cute boots. And you will think, "I'm not ready. I need to do more praying, asking, and researching."

As soon as that thought comes to you, calm is restored. So you assume that must be the wise thing to do. But that's not true. It's the *safe* thing to do. But God-sized dreams aren't about being safe. They are about holy risk, leaps of faith, putting yourself out there and into the hands of God, where you know that unless he comes through, you will fall.

When that fear hits, when you want to take a step back . . . go forward instead. Tell yourself,

"I don't know everything. But I know enough. And more importantly, I know the God who does know it all. I trust him to guide me."

When you do that, your heart will still pound—just maybe not quite as hard.

Your mind will still swirl—but maybe now with a bit of excitement mixed in too. Your knees will still knock—but your feet will be standing on solid ground.

And, most importantly, your faith will begin to be in charge rather than your fear. We want it to be easier. We want to get rid of fear and *then* take steps forward in faith. But it simply doesn't work that way in the kingdom.

You have to take the first step when you're still afraid. And when God comes through for you, your fear will shrink just a bit. The next time it will get a bit smaller again. All the while, your faith will grow.

Faith is experiential. That means we have to live it and not just think about it. As Scripture says, "Faith without deeds is dead" (James 2:26). And I would say that "fear with deeds is dead too." You can't kill fear instantly. You can only starve it by feeding your faith.

All of those questions that begin with "What if . . ." are scraps you're feeding your fear. Replace them instead with "What then . . ."

> What, then, shall we say in response to these things? If God is for us, who can be against us? He who did not spare his own Son, but gave him up for us all—how will he not also, along with him, graciously give us all things? . . . In all these things we are more than conquerors through him who loved us. For I am convinced that neither death nor life, neither angels nor demons, neither the present nor the future, nor any powers, neither height nor depth, nor anything else in all creation, will be able to separate us from the love of God that is in Christ Jesus our Lord.
>
> Romans 8:31–32, 37–39

You have what you need to take the next step. You will never feel ready but God has promised you all you need to move forward in faith. Leave the doubts behind and go with him.

All the way to your dream.

Explore

Slowly reread Romans 8:31–32 and 37–39 in the devotional above.

Express

God, you are the one who makes me more than a conqueror no matter what I may face. Thank you that whatever you call me to, you will equip me for too. Sometimes my God-sized dream can seem scary, and I want to hold back. But I choose to step forward in faith and trust that you will provide everything I need along the way. Amen.

Experience

What is the next small step you can take for your God-sized dream? Try to think of something you can do today that will take fifteen minutes or less. Now go do it. Yep, right now.

Opening the Door to Your God-Sized Dream

4

The Secret No One Tells You

Take delight in the LORD,
and he will give you the desires of
your heart.

Psalm 37:4

A summer camp sky spreads above me. I'm in junior high and spending a few nights away from home. As I stare up at the stars, my little heart is already filled with longings for the future—to get married one day, to be a writer, to have someone to sit with at the lunch table. As I thank God for my blessings and express my desires, it seems I hear a whisper . . .

Always remember to love the Giver more than the gift.

I know instantly what those words mean. I've seen how easily my childish heart can look at God like a vending machine. But he's beckoning me into intimacy instead. Through the years whenever a dream or desire comes into being, that phrase echoes in my heart again.

Love the Giver more than the gift.

We have high hopes for our God-sized dreams. We think they'll bring us joy, chase away our insecurities, soothe our fears. But there is only One who can do those things: the Giver.

We sometimes forget that truth on the road to our dreams. We start chasing what we want instead of the One who wanted us enough to come all the way from heaven to earth. Keri Lynn shares her struggle with this when she says:

Yes, I have been guilty of pursuing the dream instead of the Dream Giver. I have been guilty of following my heart instead of searching for his. . . . It's not that God doesn't want us to pursue our dreams; he does! After all, he is the one who put the dream in our hearts. He wants to dream with us, to be the one whispering in our ear and holding our hand as we walk the path he's set before us.

Yes, I'm a dreamer. But he is my dream. Knowing him, loving him, serving him, following him; that is the dream I must pursue. And as I draw closer to him, as my heart longs for more of him, I hear him quietly whisper in my ear, "turn here," "call her," "ask him," "knock on this door." And step by step, hand in hand, he leads me closer to my heart's desire.[1]

The secret no one tells you about your dreams is this: they are nothing more than a shadow of the One you truly want. He is your joy. He is your peace. He is your hope and confidence. Everything you're longing for is ultimately found in him.

Then why do our dreams matter? Because they are the path we walk with him. The journey that leads us closer to his heart. The way we experience life with the One who gave it to us.

Here's the wonderful truth hidden within that as well: *if you chase the Giver, then you will always get what you want in the end*—even if the God-sized dream you imagined doesn't turn out to meet your expectations. You can't fail when you are pursuing him, because he promises, "You will seek me and find me when you seek me with all your heart" (Jer. 29:13).

Pause for a moment and take a deep breath. Ask yourself if your God-sized dream has its proper place in your life. If not, tell God you want him to be the center of your desires again. He loves you so much that he will never let you settle for anything less than his heart.

God-sized dreams make beautiful gifts but terrible idols. Only the Giver can offer us what we truly need, what our hearts have wanted all along.

Love the Giver more than the gift.

Explore

Read Psalm 37. What other truths about God-sized dreams do you see?

Express

God, you are the Giver of all that's good—including the God-sized dreams in my heart. I recognize you are the true fulfillment of all I long for and truly need. Thank you for the invitation to go on this adventure not because of where it will take me but because of the joy of sharing it with you. I look forward to growing closer to you along the way. Amen.

Experience

Write "Love the Giver more than the gift" on a tag and stick it on a bag or small wrapped box. Then set it out somewhere so you can see it this week.

5

The Backstory to Your God-Sized Dream

Do not dwell on the past.
See, I am doing a new thing!

Isaiah 43:18–19

We all have a backstory.

You do.

I do too.

I don't talk about mine much. But I thought as we get started together I should tell you a few things. Because it might be tempting to come here and think that the road to where I am now has been easy. Or that I have it all together. Or that all my God-sized dreams have happened. But none of those are true.

In reality, I've struggled off and on with depression and social anxiety most of my life.

My husband and I have walked through many, many years of infertility, and we have a baby in heaven.

God asked me to leave a job with people I loved and take a step of faith without having any idea what would happen.

I still have days when I feel crazy and wonder what in the world I'm doing, and the fear doesn't just knock but *bangs* on the door of my heart.

You see, God-sized dreams aren't about being perfect. Or getting what we want. Or things working out the way we plan. Melanie Self said it this way:

> The journey to our destination has not always been one paved with joy, smiles, and bliss. It has taken me to many dark and difficult places in body, mind, and spirit but in every situation I have found redemption in the Father's love, leading, and plan. I LOVE sharing

his story of redemption in my life. It is never too late to start. To be faithful. To believe. To Dream. God continues to quietly call to us, drawing us closer and speaking to the Spirit of God alive and active in our hearts.[1]

I can tell you this, on your God-sized dreams journey . . .

You will feel fear.
You will fail at some point.
And you may even find that you have to let a dream go.

But I can also tell you, on your God-sized dreams journey . . .

You will become more courageous.
You will have victories you never thought possible.
And you will be filled up with what you really need, which is less of you and more of Jesus in your life.

God-sized dreaming isn't for wimps.
But at the same time it's really *only* for wimps.

Because we all are exactly that. We're weak and broken and afraid. And we're also strong and whole and filled with the resurrection power of Christ.

We are living paradoxes, and nothing will show you that more than a God-sized dream.

If you're looking at all this God-sized dreams stuff with a bit of skepticism, let me just whisper, "It's okay to feel that way. But dare to come with us anyway. Not because of where you will go but because of where this journey will take you . . . and that's closer to the heart of God."

Dare to turn the page on your backstory.

It's time for a new beginning.

Explore

Read about God's desire to help you move forward in Isaiah 43:1–19.

Express

God, I love that one of your names is "I am." That means you are always present with me in the here and now. I want to embrace this moment with you and move forward too. I ask that you would help me not dwell on the past. Redeem it and turn it into something that can be used for your glory. Amen.

Experience

Is there anything in your past holding you back from your God-sized dream? If so, write it on a piece of paper and destroy it—shred it, burn it (safely, please), throw it away. It's a new day for you and your dream.

6

Embrace Your Gifts

*Each of you should use whatever gift
you have received to serve others, as
faithful stewards of God's grace in its
various forms.*

1 Peter 4:10

We already talked about loving the gift more
than the Giver as one way our hearts can stray.
When we do that, we make our God-sized dream
an idol. On the opposite extreme, we can pre-
tend our gifts don't exist at all. Oh, we usually
have good intentions when we do so. After all,

wouldn't acknowledging that we have gifts be prideful?

And yet gratitude for what we've been given always puts us in a position of humility, not pride. *It's okay to recognize and even celebrate what God has placed within you.*

I explored this in detail through the books *You're Already Amazing* and *You're Made for a God-Sized Dream*, so let's just quickly revisit some of the ways God shows how wonderful he is through you.

First, let's talk about your strengths. Those are personal characteristics placed within you by God that can be used to serve others. For example, "encouraging" or "organized" would each be a strength.

What is one of your strengths? List it below.

When we express our strengths through our actions, those are our skills. For example, maybe you encourage through the skill of writing, or you might help others get organized by managing projects.

What is one of your skills? List it below.

Your strengths and skills are gifts God has placed within you that you can offer to the world. They are the heart of your God-sized dream. Because without them, your dream would forever remain just an idea.

I've heard many women say, "I can't focus on who I am. It's selfish." But actually choosing to understand and embrace who you are is one of the most unselfish things you can do because it maximizes your ability to serve others and bring glory to God.

What can you thank God for about who you are? Push your insecurity aside for a moment and ask him to help you see it. Give yourself permission to pause and declare with the psalmist, "I am fearfully and wonderfully made" (Ps. 139:14).

Here's another reason this is so important: if we don't acknowledge who God has made us and thank him for it, then our God-sized dreams can be what we look toward to heal our insecurity. And I can tell you from experience that doesn't work! Yes, God-sized dreams help us become more of who we're created to be, but they can never fill that identity hole within us.

We can think, "This God-sized dream will give me what I need."

God invites us to say instead, "God has given me what I need, so now I will share it through this God-sized dream."

When you can embrace that truth, then pursuing a God-sized dream becomes about joy, because you really have nothing to lose. You've already been given what matters most, and no one can take it away.

What gifts are waiting to be opened within your heart? How will you use them to change your little corner of the world today?

Explore

Read 1 Peter 4:1–11 to find out more about serving others.

Express

God, thank you for creating me with gifts. I'm grateful for the strengths that you've placed within me and the ways those are expressed as actions through my skills. I humbly acknowledge that I do have something to offer and that you have made me to make a difference. Amen.

Experience

Go to www.holleygerth.com and on the Books & More page download the interactive tools document for *You're Already Amazing* (it's free). On page 2 you'll find a list that will help you discover more of your strengths, and on page 4 there's one for your skills.

7

When You Don't Feel Worthy of Your Dream

*Because of the L*ORD*'s great love we*
are not consumed,
for his compassions never fail.
They are new every morning;
great is your faithfulness.

Lamentations 3:22–23

The new day slips fingers of light around the curtains in my bedroom and taps me gently on the shoulder. In response, I pull the covers back over my head. I don't want to face this day. I don't want to do this dream. I don't want to come out from my cave of protective pillows.

Scenes from the night before flash through my mind. How could I have done that? How could I have said that? And, most importantly, how could God ever want to use me again after I failed so miserably?

I can almost see the news ticker flashing across the ceiling: Christian author acts like a fool and is fired forever by Jesus. I groan and turn over to dig deeper into the sheets. Have you ever had a moment like this? If you haven't yet, you will. At some point the reality that you are completely unworthy of your God-sized dream will hit you right in the heart.

Because God has this funny tendency. He chooses messy, broken people to do extraordinary, God-glorifying things.

An adulterer to lead his holy nation (David).
A prostitute in the lineage of the Messiah (Rahab).
An accomplice to murder to spread the gospel (Paul).

Even Peter, one of the disciples, denied Jesus three times on the night before he went to the cross. Can you imagine what Peter thought when he woke up the next day?

I don't know how to explain this part of how God works. It's so different than how we as humans would do it. We would choose the most perfect among us, the steadiest, the least risky. But God scandalously and stubbornly chooses sinners instead.

The real danger to your God-sized dream is not failure. God took care of that on the cross through Christ. No, *the deepest threat to your God-sized dream is that you will believe the lie that you must be worthy*. Let's settle that here and now. You're not worthy. I'm not worthy. A God-sized dream isn't something we're qualified for—it's something we're called to in spite of ourselves.

In humility we respond, "God, I know I'm a mess. But I believe somehow you can use me anyway. I offer myself to you just as I am today. And I will again tomorrow. No matter what mistakes I make. No matter how many times I fall down. I will get back up and serve you forever."

Until we are in heaven, we will not be perfect. Yes, we are to seek obedience because we love our Master. But he wants to use us even when we fall short.

I finally lift the covers off my head. As I do, I feel the weight of guilt slip away too. I breathe in forgiveness, mercies that are new every morning, and say hello again to my God-sized dream. I don't know how this day will go. But I do know where I can always go when I need grace.

Are you feeling unworthy of your dream today? Do you wonder how God could even want you when he knows everything about you? Push aside those lies and doubts, the fears and failures, and take hold again of the One who will never let you go. Then welcome this day with courage, faith, and the belief that nothing you do (or don't do) can overcome his love for you.

Explore

Read Lamentations 3:19–33 about God's mercy for messy people.

Express

God, you know everything about me. My past, my present, and my future are all in your sight. There are things I wish were different. I ask forgiveness for the ways I have fallen short, and I receive your grace. Thank you that your mercies are new every morning and that you will keep making me more like Christ until the day I'm home with you forever. Amen.

Experience

What has been making you feel unworthy of your dream? Write out Lamentations 3:22–23 and set it next to your alarm clock so it's the first thing you see each morning this week.

Opening the Door to Your God-Sized Dream

8

Use What You've Already Got

David fastened on his sword over the tunic and tried walking around, because he was not used to them. "I cannot go in these," he said to Saul, "because I am not used to them." So he took them off.

1 Samuel 17:39

As soon as you speak your God-sized dream out loud, people will have helpful advice for you. "Here's what worked for me," they will say. Or perhaps, "Read this book to find the right way."

Maybe even, "Unless you do this, it's not going to work."

While well-intentioned, those remarks can begin to weigh on our hearts. We can start to question what we're doing or how we're pursuing our God-sized dream. "These are people I respect," we tell ourselves, "so they must know what I'm supposed to do."

This dilemma isn't new for God-sized dreamers. All the way back in ancient Israel we find a young shepherd boy who will one day be king struggling with the same thing. David has come to visit his brothers on the battle lines only to find that a giant on the side of the enemy is taunting the troops and mocking God. A dream is born in his heart—to defend the honor of his nation and faith.

David tells King Saul that he will fight Goliath, even though the mightiest men are standing back with knees knocking. Saul evaluates this young man and decides he doesn't have what it takes to make this dream happen. So he does what so many people in our lives do when they look at us too: he offers David his armor.

Initially, David accepts. After all, Saul is the king. His armor is the best! Surely this must be the way to accomplish the God-sized dream of taking down Goliath. But after trying what Saul says will work, David draws a different conclusion. "I cannot go in these," he says, "because I am not used to them" (1 Sam. 17:39). David lays down the armor and takes up what God has given him instead—a sling and some stones. What he already has seems the most unlikely choice for this God-sized dream, but it's all he truly needs.

David has spent years training for this moment without even realizing it. Perhaps he sat under the stars in lonely fields asking God, "Why can't I learn to be a soldier like my brothers? I want to be used by you, but I have no sword. I only have this sling and these stones. How can I ever bring you glory with those?" And perhaps God smiled back from the heavens knowing that the very things that seemed so ordinary to David would one day be exactly what he needed to bring extraordinary victory to God's people.

What if David had listened to Saul? Perhaps he still would have won the battle. But it would have been the king's armor that got the honor rather than the King of Kings. Listen to the people in your life. Know that they are offering what they have out of love and a desire to protect you. But in the end, go with what God gives you.

People may not understand. What you have in your hands or heart may seem small or even strange to them. But that's exactly what creates the opportunity for God to do the unexpected. It sets the scene for giants to fall. For battles to be won. For God-sized dreams to come scandalously, miraculously true.

You will be given what you need to accomplish the divine purposes for your life. Nothing more and nothing less. Trust you have God's very best.

Explore

Read the whole story of David and Goliath in 1 Samuel 17. You probably heard it many times as a kid. Now look at it through the eyes of a grown-up God-sized dreamer.

Express

God, you are the source of unexpected victories. Thank you for the people in my life who offer me their armor. Please show me when this is from you and when I need to lay down those things because you have already given me what I need. Thank you that you promise to equip me with exactly what it will take to accomplish your purposes. I trust you and believe you can use me in ways beyond what I can even imagine. Amen.

Experience

Pull out a blank piece of paper. Write or sketch what others have offered to you as "armor" for your God-sized dream. Then spend time praying through them. Put a (+) by the pieces you want to keep and a (–) by those that it's time to lay down.

9

How Can You Make Time for Your God-Sized Dream?

*There is a time for everything,
and a season for every activity
under the heavens.*

Ecclesiastes 3:1

My husband flips through the channels on our television. On one, a documentary shares how time travel may one day be common in our lives. I pause for a moment and wonder what that would be like. I can think of a few friends who would love "time travel gift certificates" as future birthday gifts. Time frustrates us because we can't control it. We can manage, savor, or waste it—but we can't change it.

That leads to the question I get most often when it comes to God-sized dreams: "How can I make time for my dream?" The answer is not the one we want to hear: we can't "make" time for our God-sized dream or for anything else in our lives. God alone is the Maker of time.

What we can do is *give* time to our dreams. But that has to happen within the constraints of the clock—the 24 hours, 1440 minutes, and 86,400 seconds we have each day. There is something or someone else willing to claim every bit of that unless we intentionally say part of it has been set aside for our dreams.

Here's the good news: God-sized dreams usually don't require as much time as we think. If you're struggling to find time for your dream, start with fifteen minutes a day. If that's still too much, try five. You'll be amazed at what you can accomplish with that little bit. And if you stick to it day after day, that little will add up to a lot.

(If you want a guide to help you do so, then *The "Do What You Can" Plan* ebook can be a great resource.)

Because here's the reality: if your God-sized dream is truly from him, then there is time for it in your life. It may take some creativity, saying no to other commitments, or just plain ol' perseverance, but you can make it happen.

Sure, it would be nice to be able to move to Hawaii and focus only on our dreams. Or hire a full-time nanny. Or win the lottery. But most of us don't have those options. Our God-sized dreams have to unfold right in the middle of reality—including the reality of the ticking clock. Going slower than we like can be frustrating, but even one step forward a day is better than not moving at all.

If we're not okay with just giving a little time to our dream, then it may be that "I don't have time" isn't the real reason we're not moving ahead. Maybe the real reason is fear. Sometimes saying "I don't have time" is easier than admitting "I'm scared silly and I don't know if I can do this." Use small amounts of time as a test. If you're not willing to spend five minutes a day on your dream, then time isn't the real issue. That's okay—we all have obstacles to overcome. It's just better to know it and name it than to keep telling ourselves it's only about our schedules.

We serve the Savior who took five loaves and two fish and multiplied them into a meal that fed thousands. God can multiply our resources, including our time. We can't "make" time, but he can. Be obedient today to offer what you have, and he will be faithful to turn it into what's needed to accomplish his purposes in your life.

Explore

Read how Jesus can multiply what we have in Matthew 14:13–21.

Express

God, you are the Maker of time, and you have given me what I need to accomplish your purposes for my life. When I look at my schedule, sometimes I'm not sure how or where this dream you've placed in my heart fits, but you know. Please help me be wise with every minute that I have, and show me what you would have me do. I offer all of my life to you. Amen.

Experience

It can help to pause and do a check-in to see how we're spending our time. For one day, track your time by writing down what you do and how long each activity takes. What do you notice?

10

The Dreams Disclaimer

*Then Jesus said to his disciples,
"Whoever wants to be my disciple must
deny themselves and take up their cross
and follow me."*

Matthew 16:24

Her words pour out through a comment on my
blog. She shares how she tried to pursue a God-
sized dream only to discover that she, not Jesus,
was truly at the helm of her life. In brokenness
and difficulty, she discovered the dreams disclaimer and offered it to all of us: God-sized
dreams will ultimately mean dying to yourself.

When we set out on the road to our dreams, we may picture many things ahead. But a cross is usually not one of them. And yet it is always part of the journey. Because our God-sized dreams aren't really about us at all. They're about the kingdom, God's purposes in our generation, his refining work in our lives.

Here's the great news: after we die to ourselves, we are resurrected. For the first time ever, we can be truly alive. It's a paradox. God calls us to lay down everything and yet he offers us everything in return.

How do you know if you've died to yourself when it comes to your dream? Ask yourself, "If God asked me to lay this down and never see it come true, would I be willing to do that?" What this question gets to is this: Is obedience to God, no matter what the cost, more important to me than getting what I think I want?

It's not wrong to passionately desire to see our dreams come true. We need that fuel to move us forward. We ache and rejoice and chase hard after our dreams. And yet we also have to be willing to lay them down at any time if God says to do so.

Abraham wrestled with this when God asked him to lay his son Isaac on an altar. Isaac was a God-sized dream come true. And in ancient culture where one's son carried on the family legacy, in many ways letting go of Isaac meant Abraham had to die to himself and all his hopes too. At the last minute, God provided a ram to take the place of Isaac (a foreshadowing of what Christ would do for us). Yet Abraham had to walk through that "lay down my Isaac" moment with God.

I believe we will all do the same. In my journey of God-sized dreams, there have been specific times I know God has asked me to lay what I want most on the altar and be willing to walk away from it forever. I had to die to myself. I, too, saw him provide a "ram" in those moments—although not in the way I expected.

Other God-sized dreams have not come true, and I've had to realize those were from my flesh rather than God's heart. They needed to die so God's best for my life could truly thrive.

We serve a God of life and power. He has defeated death, and that is why he boldly asks us to die to ourselves. He knows that is not the end of the story. With him, it's only the beginning of the life we really long for and the desires of our heart coming true. In his upside-down kingdom, we die to live. And we let go of our dreams in order to really take hold of them. Are you ready to deny yourself, take up your cross, and follow the One who will lead you into more than you can even imagine?

Explore

Read how God asked Abraham to lay down his God-sized dream in Genesis 22:1–18.

Express

God, I come to you with a humble heart and say that I'm willing to lay down my God-sized dreams and even my very life for you. I know that only through doing so can I receive what is truly life and your best for me. This is hard, and I need your help. I yield to you and trust in your goodness. Amen.

Opening the Door to Your God-Sized Dream

Experience

Search your heart and ask God if there are any "Isaacs" you need to lay down. If there are, write a prayer surrendering those to him.

11

How Do You Know If This Dream Is from God?

Do not conform to the pattern of this world, but be transformed by the renewing of your mind. Then you will be able to test and approve what God's will is—his good, pleasing and perfect will.

Romans 12:2

An idea comes to mind. A longing appears in your heart. A hope finds its way into your conversations. How do you really know if it's from God?

First of all, that's a beautiful question to ask. Most people move ahead in their lives without pausing to ask what God wants. And here you are desiring to know—truly know—if this is what he has for you before you take another step. That alone is pleasing to him.

And I don't believe he wants to keep us guessing. But he also doesn't usually tell us outright what we are to do. After all, his highest goal for our journey with him is an intimate relationship, and ordering us around would make us more like robots than his beloved people. Usually, we discover what he wants us to do as we go.

In the verse above, Paul tells us we are to "test and approve" God's will. In other words, we've gotta try stuff. We don't usually like that approach. It's scary. We might mess up. We could get it wrong. And yet that is the only way for us to really know God's will—by experiencing it.

The precursor to that process is to be transformed by the renewing of our minds. In other words, to be committed to seeing our lives from

God's perspective. We do that first by being in his Word on a regular basis. Even if it doesn't have specific instructions for our situations, God can use his Spirit to illuminate what we need to see. The Bible is not a static text but rather is "alive and active" so God can use it to show us what we need for our daily lives (Heb. 4:12).

We can also ask ourselves a series of questions that help us determine whether or not this dream or opportunity is likely to be from God. These are ten questions I've found to be helpful when evaluating a decision or dream:

1. Does this fit with my strengths?

2. Does this fit with my skills?

3. Have my life experiences prepared me for it?

4. What do the people I trust most say about it?

5. Do I feel an inner tug or "leading" from God to do it?

6. Does the opportunity line up with Scripture and what I understand to be God's purpose for me?

Opening the Door to Your God-Sized Dream

7. Are there any possible "phantom reasons" that could be tempting me to say yes when God wants me to say no (e.g.: fear, guilt, a desire to please people)?

8. If I say yes, what will it mean saying no to?

9. If I say no, what will it mean saying yes to?

10. When I look back in ten years, will this be a story I want to share?

This list isn't complete, of course. But hopefully it provides a starting point for you. What other questions would you add to the list?

(Side note: one thing that's *not* on this list is, "Do I feel scared silly about doing it?" What God asks us to do often does lead to fear in the beginning. When he says "do not fear" in Scripture, it's most often to someone who is *already* afraid. If we're walking the path God has for us, then it seems fear is more often confirmation to continue than a reason to turn back. More about that tomorrow.)

After evaluating and praying, it's time to "test and approve." In other words, you move forward with what God has asked you to do to the best of your knowledge. You stay closely connected to him in the process and as you go, you adjust. If you make a mistake, you learn from it. If you clearly see his hand in something, you do more of it. God's will isn't something we see in full on one day. It's more often something we discover along the way. And in doing so, we find more of what our hearts really need—the God who wants to share every bit of the journey with us.

Explore

Read more about how God's Word can help us in Hebrews 4:12–16.

Express

God, sometimes I wish you'd send me a message with exactly what you want me to do. But I thank you that not knowing all the details leads me to be more dependent on you and helps me stay closely connected to your heart. What matters most is not what I do but that I'm sharing life with you.

Opening the Door to Your God-Sized Dream

Please guide me and help me learn to discern your will more each day.

Experience

Pick a dream or decision to evaluate and practice going through the questions above.

12

Why It's Okay That You're Scared Silly

See, the LORD your God has given you the land. Go up and take possession of it as the LORD, the God of your ancestors, told you. Do not be afraid; do not be discouraged.

Deuteronomy 1:21

Yesterday we talked about how fear is often more likely confirmation to move forward than a reason to turn back on the path to our God-sized dreams. Here's why: God wired our brains with a beautiful part called the amygdala—it controls our flight or fight response. Most of the time it works really well. For example, we instantly notice and react to the bear charging out of the woods at us.

Here's where it plays into fear being a confirmation: the amygdala likes the status quo. It sees change, especially if it means stepping out of our comfort zone, as a threat because it's unfamiliar. Therefore it registers those things as something that needs a "flight or fight response" initially.

In Scripture, when God says, "Do not fear," it is almost always to someone *already* feeling fear. He helps us get past that first response and move from fear to faith. But that first fear response is often an indicator that God is asking us to step out of our comfort zone. That's why it can be part of a confirmation that he's asking us to do something.

Your fear is not a reason to be ashamed.

And here's a secret: everyone feels afraid when they decide to pursue a God-sized dream.

I've had the privilege of walking beside thousands of women on the path to their God-sized dreams. No matter their age, location, or lifestyle, they have this in common: at some point they're scared silly. It doesn't matter if they're already a bestselling author or putting the first words ever on a page, fear still comes calling. It's no respecter of persons.

We believe a myth that goes like this: if that woman I see is successful, then she must not struggle with fear. So we hold back because we believe we have to stop being afraid before we move forward. And we certainly don't admit to anyone else that we're terrified of what may happen. But trust me on this, sisters: we're all in this together.

Just this morning I stared at the computer screen and felt the familiar prickle at the back of my neck that said, "If you try that, something terrible will happen." Thankfully, I've been at this long enough now to realize that fear is quite the exaggerator. I can brush off those feelings a bit more easily than when I first began, but they're still present.

When psychologists want to help a client overcome a phobia, one of the most effective treatments is exposure therapy. Little by little, bit by bit, they safely enable the client to confront what frightens them. Each time that happens, the client's brain (specifically, the amygdala) learns to lower the threat alert level for that particular thing. It's the same way with us. We can't talk ourselves out of fear. We just have to take steps of faith so that we can see we really are going to be okay. Then our brain gets on board and the "sound the alarm" sensation of fear gets quieter over time.

God understands your fear. He doesn't condemn you for it or tell you to snap out of it. Instead he takes you by the hand and speaks to your heart words of courage, love, and grace. Lean in and listen to his voice until it's louder than the fear.

You can pursue your God-sized dream with him by your side—even if you're afraid.

Explore

The Israelites chose to obey fear rather than moving forward in faith in spite of their fear. Read what that did to their God-sized dream of entering the Promised Land in Deuteronomy 1:26–37.

Express
....

God, thank you for creating me with the ability to feel fear. Without that capability, it would be difficult for me to survive in this world. Yet I don't want to give fear more of a place in my life than you ever intended it to have. I choose today not to live in ongoing fear or let it hold me back from taking steps of faith. Please give me courage as I move forward with you. Amen.

Experience
....

What is your worst fear about your God-sized dream? Defuse its power over you by daring to speak it out loud to someone you trust, and then replace those words with what God says instead.

13

You're Never a Failure

*I will become even more undignified
than this, and I will be humiliated in
my own eyes.*

2 Samuel 6:22

The coffee shop is quiet except for the sound of voices at the table across from me, and I can't help but overhear.

An older man says, "Most people think failure is here." He taps one edge of the table. "And that success is here." He taps the opposite edge. Then he places both of his hands in the center of the

....
77

table. "But failure and success are really here. Side by side."

The young man he's talking to nods and the mentor continues, "Don't try to avoid failure completely. Or you'll never be successful."

His words ring in my ears and my heart as I take another sip of coffee.

Every time I get ready to try something new I hear the question, "What if it doesn't work?" And the answer is, of course, "I'll look like a fool." Over time I've come to believe this—*that's not a good enough reason not to do it.*

Sometimes looking like a fool comes with the territory of God-sized dreams.

Noah built an ark.

Moses wandered in the desert.

Jesus hung on the cross.

And those who watched shook their heads and muttered words like "failure" and "fool."

Little did they know.

Is that you today?

Have you stepped out in faith and wondered why you feel like a fool?

Opening the Door to Your God-Sized Dream

Have you come across failure like a roadblock in your path?

Keep going, friend.

Instead of fleeing from the feeling of being foolish, lean into it. King David did this when the Ark of God entered Jerusalem. He danced in joy with lots of abandon and little clothing in front of the people. His wife scolded him for what she saw as inappropriate behavior for a person of his position. I love his response: "I will become even more undignified than this, and I will be humiliated in my own eyes." Where most of us would apologize and try to defend ourselves, David essentially says: "You ain't seen nothing yet." He realizes that defending his honor is not his job and that God gets the most glory when we humble ourselves.

If you're not willing to look goofy in the eyes of others at some point, you will never make it to your God-sized dream.

And what seems like your most foolish moments may turn out to be your wisest. As Jim Elliot said, "He is no fool who gives what he cannot keep to gain what he cannot lose."[1]

It turns out when you feel lowest, you may actually be higher than you can even know.

From that unexpected place, you'll be able to see what true success means.

Feel it.

Know it.

Reach out and touch its nail-scarred hands.

Don't give up. Or give in. Or compromise. Or quit.

You're going to make it.

And it's going to make you . . .

not into a fool,

not into a failure,

but into a victorious follower.

Explore

Read about David dancing like a fool in 2 Samuel 6:12–22.

Opening the Door to Your God-Sized Dream

Express

God, thank you that I don't have to try to gain the approval of other people. Because of you, I am free to be a "fool" in the eyes of the world. When it seems to others I'm failing, that may be the very time when you are working most powerfully in my life. Help me to look to you for my identity and security. Amen.

Experience

Think of one thing you're afraid to do when it comes to your God-sized dream because you're worried you'll look silly if it doesn't work. Now do it anyway. Yep, today.

14

Why We Need
You to Shine

You are the light of the world.

Matthew 5:14

A gunman walks into an elementary school and
takes the lives of twenty innocent children. As I
write these words, the world is still reeling from
the shock and tragedy of the Newtown, Connecti-
cut, school shooting. I click through photos of the
lives that ended far too soon and fixate on one.
Emilie Parker. Six years old. Blonde hair and the
heart of an encourager. She had already started

making cards for family members and friends when they were hurting. She could have been me. I could have been her.

I wrestle with this as I stare at the ceiling in the night. I want to understand the darkness. I want to grasp it so I can hurl it away forever.

But that's not how darkness works. We can't go after it directly. That's like chasing a shadow. The only way to decrease darkness is to add more light.

And you are the light of the world (Matt. 5:14).

I shared that on my blog, and a reader responded that Jesus is the light of the world. And, yes, he is. But in one of those God-paradoxes, he chooses to shine through us. If we want this world to become brighter, we are the ones who must do it.

That's why we need your God-sized dream.

We can get caught up in analyzing the darkness and trying to figure it out. Right now there are endless theories on why the school shooting happened. I don't know the answer. And we may never know. And while these are important discussions to have for those who can influence the issues involved, for most of us it has come back to this: "What can I personally do about this today?"

I don't know the specifics of the answer, but here's the part that applies to all of us: we can shine where we are today.

You can use your gifts.
You can serve those around you.
You can love God in your everyday life.
You can pursue the dream he's placed in your heart.

When you do those things, you flip on the light switch. And who knows how far the glow will go?

One thing that grieves my heart (and I think God's too) is how many times as believers we sit around talking with each other about the darkness in our world. It seems we think by being aware of the darkness and saying we don't like it that we're actually changing something. But we're not. If we say we're passionate about an issue or need, we must take action. And here's the thing: we can talk about almost anything, but I believe we're called to a specific something.

Your God-sized dream probably started with darkness. You saw a need in our world, and you felt called to meet it. The temptation is to stay in the dark, feeling sad about it. But at some point we have to just go out and shine. The best way we can. With what God has given us. Right where we are.

Emilie Parker did that in her six years of life. It's not about the time we have but how we use it—how faithful we are with what we've been given.

When we all shine, we begin to crowd out the darkness.

Dare to be the light of the world.

Together we can make this world brighter.

We need you, and your God-sized dream, more than ever.

Explore

Read more about how you can be the light of the world in Matthew 5:14–16.

Express

God, I praise you because you are the true light, yet you have chosen to shine through us. I embrace this role and ask you to show me how I can do so right here, right now. Sometimes the darkness can seem overwhelming, but light overcomes darkness every time. Help me to decrease the darkness in this world by adding more light. Amen.

Experience

Go into a room of your house and try to remove the darkness. Can you find any other way to do it besides adding more light?

Opening the Door to Your God-Sized Dream

15

On Dating
Your Dreams

Sow your seed in the morning,
*   and at evening let your hands not*
*   be idle,*
for you do not know which will
*   succeed,*
*   whether this or that,*
*   or whether both will do equally well.*

Ecclesiastes 11:6

She slides into the seat at the lunch table and
declares, "I've found *The One!*" with a gleam in

her eyes. She tells me about the new boy sitting next to her in biology class and how she's certain they'll live happily ever after. I smile and shake my head. There's a new crush every week. Years later, as I gush about how beautiful she looks in her wedding gown, she giggles and says, "Aren't you glad I didn't marry any of those other boys? I guess you have to go through a lot of frogs to find your prince!"

A friend slides into a seat at our favorite coffee shop and declares, "I've found *The One*!" with a gleam in her eyes. She tells me about the new dream that has come into her life and how she's certain this time it will last forever. I smile and shake my head. There's a new idea every week. Years later as I gush about how finding her true calling has given her a glow of joy, she giggles and says, "Aren't you glad I didn't stick with any of those other dreams?" I nod—I'm really glad for all the dreams I dated and then left behind too.

We all want to find *The One* and to do it *right now*. But saying that we're going to find the greatest God-sized dream of our lives, recognize it instantly, and pursue it without interference is like marrying the boy in our sixth-grade science

Opening the Door to Your God-Sized Dream

class. It happens, but it's rare. More often we discover our dreams through a long and twisty-turny process. *And that's okay.*

We need to give ourselves permission to explore. And if what we thought would be the dream for our lives turns out not to be, we need to see that as a step forward, not as a failure.

We all have desires swirling around in our hearts. We hope or pray or have a vision. Then we wonder, "But is this really it? Is this *the one*?"

For most of us, those questions sound familiar. They're the same ones we asked when looking for true love in our lives. So what do we do?

Date.

Because that cute boy we have our eye on in biology class may turn out to be completely incompatible with us.

We can use the same approach with our dreams.

For example, if you dream of starting an orphanage, then begin by working in the nursery of your church.

If you think you want to become a musician, then give free concerts at a local coffeehouse.

Want to write a book? Start a blog.

Whatever your *big dream* is, think of a smaller version and date it first.

We even see this a lot in Scripture. Before David became leader of Israel, he led a flock of sheep. Before Peter fished for the souls of men, he spent time literally casting nets into the sea.

If you feel a lot of hesitation about doing so, that's a red flag. Here's why: it may be that you're drawn to your dream because in your mind it's this perfect reality. If you just make it come true, then you will live happily ever after. But it never, ever works that way. Even God's dreams for us are filled with challenges and obstacles too. *Your dream needs to brush up against reality before you commit to it.* And that's exactly what dating your dream lets you do.

Dream dating lets you explore what the future you're considering is really like.

How it lines up with your strengths and skills.

And it gives you time to ask God those important questions, "Is this really it? Is this *the one*?"

Because here's the thing: we're never meant to answer those questions ourselves. It's God who

Opening the Door to Your God-Sized Dream

gets to tell us the dreams we're meant to be with for life. But we've got to give him that chance by taking some steps forward.

So go ahead, date your dreams.

You may walk away feeling relieved you never have to go out with some of them again. Or you just may discover a love of your life.

What dream would you like to date?

Explore

See more about embracing opportunities in Ecclesiastes 11:1–6.

Express

God, I'm so glad that I have the freedom to "date" my dreams. I want to ultimately find what you want me to be deeply committed to for life. So I ask for discernment and that you would help my heart be drawn to what you truly want me to pursue. Give me wisdom and direct me into your will. Amen.

On Dating Your Dreams

Experience

Next time you're around little girls who are just starting to have crushes on boys, ask them some questions about who they think they'll marry one day. Let it remind you of how innocently inaccurate our perspective can be about the future and how we need time and experience to test our theories about what's best for us.

16

When You're Just Not Feeling It

Let us not become weary in doing good,
for at the proper time we will reap a
harvest if we do not give up.

Galatians 6:9

She sends me an email.

Or walks up to me at a conference.

Maybe whispers it across the table at lunch.

It starts with something like, "I know I'm called to write or speak or cook or do spreadsheets"— her voice gets lower here—"but what about the days when I'm just not feeling it?"

I nod. Because I know. *Oh, how I know.*

What I don't know is how our culture has convinced us that any other skill is okay to practice, but if it's spiritual or art or both, then you have to feel it every time.

As I'm writing this, the Olympics are still fresh on our minds. I'm picturing an interviewer asking an athlete, "How often do you practice?" And the reply being, "When I feel like it."

We don't ever hear that from athletes at that level.

As Aristotle said, "We are what we repeatedly do. Excellence, therefore, is not an act but a habit."

What do you do when you don't feel it? You do it anyway.

It's different if you don't know what God wants you to do. But if you know that words, or food, or corporate work is your thing, *then you do it.* Over and over again.

That's stewardship—which really just means taking good care of what you've been given and making the most of it.

So if guilt has been chasing you around and yelling in your ear about how you can't do something unless you really feel it, then it's time to kick guilt to the curb.

Then do your dream.

Do it today.

Do it tomorrow.

Do it for the rest of your life.

Your God-sized dream is just as much about perspiration as inspiration. In the early stages, when we're filled with enthusiasm and passion, it's easy to take action. But at some point that will begin to subside or life will get busy or the dog will eat our business plan. And we will begin to think, "Maybe I'll do something else."

Now we just talked about "dating" our dreams. So let's clarify the difference: If you try a dream and realize it's not truly a fit with who God has created you to be and what God has called you to do, then move on. That's wisdom. But if you're "breaking up" with a dream just because you're bored or don't feel the same way you did in the beginning, then think twice. There is no such thing as a God-sized dream that doesn't have seasons that are just plain ol' hard, unglamorous work.

When we persevere through those times, we honor God, because that is when we're dying to ourselves. We're saying, "I will obey even when all

When You're Just Not Feeling It

my flesh wants to do is sit in the corner and eat a cookie." When you choose to be disciplined in the pursuit of your dream, even when you don't want to, you do a lot to destroy the work of the enemy. And even though it doesn't feel like it, your faith is probably even stronger than when you have all the warm, fuzzy emotions that we like a lot better.

So keep going, friend.

You're doing better than you know.

You're growing more than you realize.

You're making a difference even if you can't see it.

And someday soon, you will.

Explore

Read more about perseverance and the rewards that come with it in Galatians 6:7–10.

Express

God, thank you that I can bring you joy and be obedient even when my emotions don't line up

*with what my heart truly desires. I choose to die
to myself and embrace your will for me. I will continue to do what you've asked me to, whether or
not I feel it. And I trust that as I do, you will bring
forth new life and growth in ways I can't even
imagine. Amen.*

Experience

Plant a seed in a small pot, and water it each
day as a reminder that faithfulness, even when
we can't see or feel the growth, can eventually
make a big difference.

17

When It Looks Like
Your Dream Has
Kicked the Bucket

*So neither the one who plants nor the
one who waters is anything, but only
God, who makes things grow.*

1 Corinthians 3:7

In the "Experience" section of the last devotional
I suggested that you plant a seed and water it
as a reminder of what faithfulness, even without
feelings, can bring forth in your life. And now
I must make a confession to you: I am a plant

assassin. Yes, ma'am. If there's a plant in your life you would like to die, just give it to me, and I will have it taken care of in no time.

In spite of that, last summer I did a very brave thing. I bought a tomato plant. To understand why that's an act of courage, let me share my history of plants with you one more time. Don't worry, we've already covered most of it, and I can sum it all up in three little words:

I kill them.

Every few years I decide to change my wicked, plant-hit-woman ways. I wander into a store for completely unrelated reasons and there they are . . . rows of promising little pots just begging to be taken home (well, in my case they are probably hollering for me to leave them there).

This year I yielded to temptation and picked up a cherry tomato plant.

I put it in the sunshine.

I watered it.

Sometimes I forgot.

Then I went out of town.

I came home and my little plant had turned the color of crispy French fries. "Too bad," I said to myself. "Another one bites the dust." I felt a bit disappointed because this time I really tried. I watered that thing. I put it in the sun. I even talked to it and told it what a good little plant it was.

I strolled across the yard with sorrow in my southern heart. But when I got to that plant, I stopped right in my tracks.

Lo and behold, two bright red tomatoes smiled up at me.

I clapped my hands. Not only had my crispy plant managed to survive, it had just grown my very first tomatoes.

I carried those tomatoes into the house and showed my husband. I took pictures of them. I put them on Facebook.

My little dream had somehow managed to come true in spite of my shortcomings.

That's often how it works. We set out with good intentions. Then life interferes, we forget to water, we go out of town, and we think the dream is surely done. But all the while God is

Opening the Door to Your God-Sized Dream

still working in mysterious ways beyond our understanding.

If you have a dream that looks like crispy French fries in the sun, don't give up yet. Because you just never know. Sometimes when we least expect it, when we don't deserve it, when we can hardly believe it . . . everything changes.

My little plant has two more tomatoes on it. They're still green, and I'm watching, waiting, seeing the "impossible" grow before my eyes.

Yes, we are to try our best to "water" and persevere in what we do with our dreams. But at some point, we will fail. Instead of giving up, we can rely on God to make things grow in spite of us.

If your dream has gotten a little wilted, don't give up yet.

Look for growth and get back to work on it.

You never know when the best is yet to be.

Explore

Read more about how God is the true source of all growth in 1 Corinthians 3:6–8.

Express

God, I'm committed to being faithful with what you've given me to take care of in my life. Yet I know in the end that you alone create real life and growth. When my dream seems to be wilting, please help it to continue in spite of my shortcomings. I yield the results to you and look forward to what you will bring forth. Amen.

Experience

Find a fruit or vegetable in your house and have a healthy snack. As you do, think about all the growth it took and obstacles that had to be overcome just for that good food to come to you.

18

What to Do
While You're Waiting
On Your Dreams

*There is a time for everything,
and a season for every activity
under the heavens.*

Ecclesiastes 3:1

When we start pursuing a dream, we have a time-
line in mind. We may even pull out a calendar
and circle the due date. We imagine what it will
be like to finally live in our new reality. Then our
deadline comes and goes, and we're still waiting.

Huh.

What now?

My husband and I experienced this when we decided to have children. We wanted to start a family right away, but God had other plans. Over seven years later, we've done our share of learning to wait. In the process God has transformed that original dream of having physical children into new and unexpected hopes and plans in our lives. But I don't think that would have been possible if we hadn't discovered a few things about waiting well.

1. *Get wise advice.* As I mentioned above, I've spent a lot of time waiting in the last few years. And I keep hoping God will start using email. Then I'll just get up every morning, and his agenda will be sitting in my inbox.

    While that hasn't happened yet, I have noticed that words from wise people in my life (through email or otherwise) often do lead me to the answer God has for me.

    Don't be afraid to ask others for their perspective. "Victory is won through many advisers" (Prov. 11:14).

Opening the Door to Your God-Sized Dream

2. *Pay attention to the details.* I'm a big-picture kind of girl. I think God should do the whole "handwriting on the wall" thing more often, don't you?

   But it seems uncovering his will is often more like connect-the-dots. So when I'm in seasons of waiting, I journal more. I write down every little thing that I think he's saying to me. Over time, a pattern often emerges that I wouldn't have seen otherwise. *It's often the little things that lead us to the big ones.*

3. *Don't put the rest of your life on hold.* When I'm waiting on God in one area, sometimes I come to a screeching halt in every area of my life. *But it's hard to steer a parked car.*

   Sometimes we find what we're waiting on along the way—not when we stay. I love how Isaiah 40:31 says those who wait on the Lord will run and not grow weary and walk and not faint. *There can still be a lot of movement going on during the waiting.*

4. *Forget the fear.* Sometimes we think we're "waiting on God" when really we're just waiting for the fear to go away. Here's a

hint: *it won't*. The enemy will tell you that courage means the absence of fear as you move ahead. *It doesn't*.

Faith means feeling the fear and moving ahead into God's will anyway. (Remember Jesus sweating drops of blood before he went to the cross?)

5. *Be grateful for where you are.* Oh, friend, I'm t-e-r-r-i-b-l-e at this one. Yep. I like to move on to the next thing. I look ahead and forget to enjoy and appreciate where I am today.

Sometimes I need to stop and remember that *I'm living today in the answered prayers of yesterday*. And that is reason to say a big ol' "thank you" a lot more often than I do.

God's timing is not like ours. Sometimes we face delays and detours we never expected. While those can be discouraging, they can also lead to gifts along the way we never would have discovered otherwise.

When it comes to our God-sized dreams, we may not know when we will arrive—but we can always be sure God will be by our side giving us what our hearts really need. Today. Tomorrow. Forever.

Explore

Read more about timing and life's seasons in Ecclesiastes 3:1–8.

Express

God, your timing is not like mine. Sometimes it's hard to be patient. I yield to your divine schedule. Show me when to speed up, when to slow down, and when to simply be still. Most of all, I want to share each moment of my life with you. Amen.

Experience

Sometimes we don't even realize we've set a "deadline" for our God-sized dream. Have you done so? Look at your personal calendar—the one on the wall or just in your heart. What adjustments might need to be made?

19

When Your God-Sized Dream Gets Hard

Now if we are children, then we are heirs—heirs of God and co-heirs with Christ, if indeed we share in his sufferings in order that we may also share in his glory.

Romans 8:17

Sara Frankl spent the last years of her life confined by the walls of her home due to a debilitating medical condition. Still a young woman, she had to face that many of her God-sized dreams—like marrying and raising a family—would not come true the way she imagined. And yet she held tight to the dream that mattered most to her: encouraging others with her words. She could no longer do that at an office job, but she continued to do so from her laptop at home. After Sara slipped home to Jesus, hundreds of stories of lives she had quietly and privately changed came pouring out on the internet.

I don't know what Sara imagined her life would be like when she grew up. But I'm certain the illness she faced was not part of the plan. She could have given up or given in to self-pity. Instead she persevered and chose to see her limitations as opportunities.

Henry Cloud and John Townsend say this in *How People Grow:*

Jesus turns our natural bents upside down. In the world's view, the path to glory is being "on top of it" or "having it all together." In Jesus's way, the path to glory is experiencing pain and suffering: "Now if we are children, then we are heirs—heirs of God and co-heirs with Christ, if indeed we share in his

When Your God-Sized Dream Gets Hard

sufferings in order that we may also share in his glory" (Rom. 8:17).[1]

When we think of God-sized dreams, it's easy to picture a path that takes us away from suffering rather than into it. Yet Scripture shows us again and again that suffering is part of the journey. That means when our God-sized dream gets hard, we don't have to say, "I must be doing something wrong." Instead we can find comfort in knowing that Christ himself faced suffering as he fulfilled his God-sized dream of redeeming the world.

This comes with a caveat: we are talking about *purposeful* suffering. Cloud and Townsend add, "He chose the path of the Cross because of the fruit it would bear for all of us. Yet he refused to enter suffering that would be inappropriate for his purposes."[2] In other words, suffering for the sake of suffering is not what God has in mind. Sometimes we go to the other extreme and believe we must suffer all the time in order to be godly. But Scripture makes it clear that God desires a life of joy for us. Suffering is intended to be temporary—whether it is resolved in this life or when we enter eternity. God wants us to thrive. Even Jesus endured the cross "for the joy set before him" (Heb. 12:2). So we are not to be surprised by suffering, and yet we're also not to simply accept it as the way things must be forever. We can ask God, "What is your purpose in this?"

You will have hard days on the road to your God-sized dream. You will face disappointments. You will experience setbacks. Yet in the middle of this you can trust that God's purposes will prevail and you are truly, deeply loved. That enables us to do what Sara did—choose joy and let nothing stand in the way of completing God's purpose for our lives.

Explore

Read Romans 8 to discover what God promises you even in the middle of hard times.

Express

God, thank you that I can trust you even in the middle of suffering. Jesus knows what it's like

to experience pain on the path to a God-sized
dream, and that's so comforting to me. I ask that
you will give me the strength, courage, and hope
I need to move forward no matter what happens
in my life. Amen.

Experience
....

Who in your life is going through a difficult time?
Send a card, make a phone call, or find another
way to share words of encouragement with that
person today.

Opening the Door to Your God-Sized Dream

20

When You Want
to Compare

Each one should test their own actions.
Then they can take pride in themselves
alone, without comparing themselves to
someone else.

Galatians 6:4

Every little girl grows up dreaming about living
in a castle. So as I flip through television channels and discover a home tour in a renovated
castle, I pause for a moment. It's gorgeous—high

walls, timeless floors, winding staircases. The hostess explains that a local architect and his wife have brought new life to this old place. The wife nods and then replies, "Would you like to see a picture of it before we began?"

What she shows the camera next almost jolts me out of my seat. *It's nothing but ruins.* No roof. No windows. Just jagged pieces of wall stretching into the sky.

I shake my head in wonder. *How did they even have a vision for what that place could be?*

Just seconds ago I thought, *It would be really cool to live in a place like that someday.* Now I take it all back. No way would I be willing to do that much work. I landed on the "happily ever after" part of that castle's story and completely missed how arduous the process had been to get there.

It's easy to do the same with the God-sized dreams of others. I look at an area of another woman's life that I admire—maybe a talent, skill, strength, or desire that has come true—and I think, *It would be really cool to live in a place like that someday.*

But I don't see the whole picture. I don't know how much renovation happened in her life to get

Opening the Door to Your God-Sized Dream

her there. I don't have the backstory that shows God gets all the glory. I haven't counted the tears or uncovered the cost along the way.

Jon Acuff shared, "Never compare your beginning to someone else's middle."[1]

I'd take it one step beyond that and say, "Never compare your middle to someone else's happy ending."

If we're longing for someone else's "castle," we're also asking for all the effort, energy, and emotion it took for that to be built in their lives. Do we really know what we're asking for?

Writer Kathryn Stockett received sixty rejection letters before a publisher accepted *The Help*, which became a runaway bestseller and popular movie.

Olympic athletes train in obscurity and make significant sacrifices just for one shot at seeing their dream come true.

The apostle Paul experienced being beaten, shipwrecked, imprisoned, and more in order to fulfill his calling.

By the time the television segment on that renovated castle finished, I felt ready to kiss my carpet.

I had a new appreciation for my realities.

So next time we see the "castle" of a God-sized dream in someone else's life, let's close our eyes for a moment and try to imagine not just what could be but what may have already been. And then take a moment to thank God for being wise enough not to give us everything we think we want—*and all that comes with it.*

Explore

Read about all the apostle Paul experienced on the way to his God-sized dream of bringing the gospel to the Gentiles in 2 Corinthians 11:22–30.

Express

God, it's so easy to look at what you have done in the life of someone else and not see all that took place along the way. Thank you that you have given me exactly what I need to complete the God-sized dreams in my heart. You are faithful and you will bring to pass your purposes for my life. Amen.

Opening the Door to Your God-Sized Dream

Experience

Think of someone you respect or admire. Then do some research and try to find out more about what they had to go through to get where they are today. What did you discover that you didn't know about before?

21

Whatever You Do, Choose Growth

Now choose life, so that you ... may live.

Deuteronomy 30:19

The snow skims the tops of the trees and drifts over the last of the leaves. It's quiet and looks like not much is happening. But I know that those trees are getting ready to grow. They'll be dormant for the winter, but deep down below new life is already coming.

I look up from my coffee and say to my

husband, "There are really only two choices in life, aren't there? Growth or decay."

It's a deep statement for a Saturday morning, but I can't shake it. Everywhere I look I see it.

Growth or decay.

Life or death.

It's always been this way. All the way back in ancient Israel, God encouraged his people, "Choose life, so that you may live" (Deut. 30:19).

And choosing life always means choosing growth too.

We're funny creatures. We want to be safe, secure, to avoid risk. When we do so, we believe that we're preserving our lives. But we're not. We're actually choosing death. To not grow is to die. There is no middle ground.

Now I don't mean taking foolish risks. What I mean is saying yes to God and moving forward with him no matter what.

Through the pain.
Through the success.
Through the struggles.
Through the victories.

Whatever you do, choose growth.

And here's the thing: like those trees, growth is not always big and flashy. It can happen quietly, almost invisibly. But it must happen.

And there's more good news: growth doesn't require perfection. In fact, it cannot coexist with it. You will fail and fall and learn and get back up again. Because that's how you grow.

I don't know where you are today, what circumstances you're facing, what this day will hold for you.

But I'm begging you, cheering for you, quietly whispering to you, "Please choose life that you may live."

The best part of all? The responsibility for growth ultimately lies with God. "God . . . makes things grow" (1 Cor. 3:7).

So you don't have to make growth happen. Your role is surrender and then obedience. When you embrace those, you can't help but grow. "That person is like a tree planted by streams of water, which yields its fruit in season and whose leaf does not wither—whatever they do prospers" (Ps. 1:3).

Opening the Door to Your God-Sized Dream

You may not be able to control what happens to you on the journey to your God-sized dreams. But you can choose how you respond to it.

Choose life.
Choose growth.
Choose God's best for you.

Explore

Read Deuteronomy 30:11–20 for more of the benefits God says come with growth.

Express

God, I choose life and growth today. When I want to hold back, help me to remember that doing so feels safe but actually takes me away from your best for me. Give me wisdom in every circumstance I face to see how I can thrive through it—even if it's not easy. I trust you to produce the fruit you want in my heart. Amen.

Experience

Take a walk today and count how many things you can find that are growing. What do they have in common? What does God reveal to us about the process of growth through the world he created?

22

What Success
Really Means

Well done, good and faithful servant!
You have been faithful with a few
things; I will put you in charge of many
things. Come and share your master's
happiness!

Matthew 25:21

We live in a world of numbers. We can measure
everything in our lives from pounds on a scale
to the amount of friends we have on Facebook.
That makes it tempting to measure the success

of our God-sized dream in a similar way too. It makes us feel safer to tell ourselves, "When I reach this specific goal, then I will be a success."

Even if we don't attach a number to it, we can still come up with other ways of being able to check the "success" box on our lives. Happy family. Flourishing career. Deep spiritual life.

Yet God calls us to see success differently. He doesn't measure or define it like we do. Rather than seeking a result, he invites us to see success as part of a relationship. To say it simply: *true success is being a good and faithful servant who brings happiness to our Master.*

> Well done, good and faithful servant! You have been faithful with a few things; I will put you in charge of many things. Come and share your master's happiness!
>
> Matthew 25:21

What does this look like in our daily lives?

First, the word *good* is about our character. It describes who we are. Thankfully, we don't have to make ourselves "good." Indeed, there's no way we even can. We're sinners who need a Savior.

Yet when we receive what Jesus did for us, we do become "good." And we bring our Master joy as we live out more and more of who we already are in him. As Paul said, "Only let us live up to what we have already attained" (Phil. 3:16).

The word "faithful" describes our actions, what we do. In other words, being faithful means being trustworthy and obedient. God can count on us to say yes to what he asks of us and to follow through on it. Will we mess up? Absolutely. What counts is that when we do, we come running back to our Master and let him help us.

In essence, success means yielding to the on-going process of Jesus transforming us in every area of our lives. When we do so, we bring him joy. It's beautiful the way this verse describes it: "enter into the joy of your master" (Matt. 25:21 NASB). In other words, the joy of the Master in his servant is *ongoing*.

Many of us go through life believing that God barely tolerates us—that he's just hanging on until we get to heaven when he can actually enjoy us. But that's not true. You can (and do) bring God joy right now.

What this also means is that if you are obedient, *you cannot fail.* Oh, it may look like it in the eyes of the world at times. But if you are faithful to your Master, then you are a success *no matter what.*

You can be a success every single day for the rest of your life. Simply get up each morning and pray, "God, I am your servant. Do with me what you will. Use me as little or as much as you want."

In ways that can't be measured, beyond what you can count or even imagine, he will answer that prayer.

And when you are home with him, you can celebrate together—forever.

Explore

Read the parable of the good and faithful servant in Matthew 25:14–30.

Express

God, I'm so grateful that you change the way we define success. I want to be a good and faithful

Opening the Door to Your God-Sized Dream

servant who brings you joy every day. I am yours. Do with me what you will. Use me as little or as much as you want. I look forward to the day when I can celebrate with you for all eternity. Amen.

Experience

None of us will be here forever. Imagine you know you are about to enter heaven and you are telling someone, "I can look back on my life with joy and know it has been a success even with all that's happened because . . ." How would you finish that sentence?

23

What a God-Sized Dream Isn't

"For my thoughts are not your
thoughts,
neither are your ways my ways,"
declares the LORD.

Isaiah 55:8

"But I thought that everything would turn out the way I planned," she says softly as she wraps her hands tighter around her coffee cup. I nod with compassion. Oh, how I've been there.

When we start the journey to a God-sized dream we often do so with many assumptions inside us. They're beliefs so deep that we usually don't even realize we're carrying them with us.

My God-sized dream will make me happy.
My God-sized dream will make me feel better about myself.
My God-sized dream will turn out the way that I expect.

Then somewhere down the road, those unspoken beliefs meet with reality and we wind up feeling frustrated, disappointed, and perhaps even a little betrayed. After all, aren't we doing what God wants?

So before you get to that point, let's have a little chat about what a God-sized dream is not.

A God-sized dream is not a path to happiness. It's a path to true joy. And that means that there is going to be suffering along the way too. "And let us run with perseverance the race marked out for us, fixing our eyes on Jesus, the pioneer and perfecter of faith. For the joy set before him he endured the cross" (Heb. 12:1–2).

A God-sized dream is not a way to feel better about ourselves. Yes, we will discover more of who we're created to be along the way. But we will also learn more about how broken, weak, and needy we are too. God-sized dreams will make you more secure in your identity in Christ, but they are not about building your "self-esteem."

A God-sized dream is not a guarantee that your expectations will be met. God's thoughts and ways are not like ours. So usually what he has in mind is different than what we imagine when we start. We can trust that we can "Take delight in the LORD, and he will give you the desires of your heart" even if it turns out those desires are actually totally different than what we first thought (Ps. 37:4).

Pause for a moment and think of the expectations attached to your God-sized dream. What do you assume will happen? What might you even believe you have a "right" to experience because you're pursuing this dream? Whatever that is, lay it at the feet of Jesus now. Tell him that you are setting aside all of what you believe a God-sized dream to be and asking for what he truly wills instead.

Your God-sized dream may not turn out to be what you have in mind.

But you can always trust that it will be what's in God's heart for you.

And there's nothing better than his best for your life.

Explore

Read Hebrews 12:1–3 to see how Jesus handled the journey to his God-sized dream of saving our world.

Express

God, it gives me so much comfort to know you understand my heart even better than I do. You can see the future and all it holds, as well as how my God-sized dream will unfold. I yield all my hopes and expectations to you. I pray, above all, that your will would be done in my life. I love you and I trust you. Amen.

Experience

Write this sentence at the top of a piece of paper: *If my God-sized dream comes true then . . .* Below that sentence, write the expectations that you have (e.g.: *I will be happy*). Ask God to search your heart and show you anything you're expecting from your dream that you may not even have realized.

24

Pursue Your Dream
with Excellence

*Do you see someone skilled in their
work?
They will serve before kings.*

Proverbs 22:29a

Imagine sitting in a doctor's office waiting for a
procedure. The surgeon walks through the door,
pulls out a butter knife, and says, "I don't have
much experience, but I feel called to medicine,
so I'm sure everything will work out all right."
You would jump right off that table and run out

the door as quick as you could. It makes sense to us that training and experience—in other words, excellence—are essential to successful surgery. Yet when it comes to our own God-sized dreams, we often tend to want to skip those parts and get right to the action.

If you are called to a God-sized dream, that is the *beginning* of the process. After you know what God is asking you to do, it's up to you to do all you can to become excellent in the area he's asking you to pursue. Sometimes that means getting a formal degree. Other times it means volunteering to gain practical experience. Or you might need mentors in your life. Whatever it is, make sure you have the tools and skills you need. Yes, God empowers you in the process too, but he wants you to put in the hard work that it takes to fully develop the potential he's placed within you.

That also means understanding *every* aspect of your God-sized dream. My grandfather owned a Christian bookstore for many years. While his store thrived, many other stores in the industry failed. Some of those belonged to his friends. I remember him saying again and again, "He wanted to do ministry, but he never learned the business part, and now he can't do either." In his eighties, my grandfather took classes to learn how to use a computer so he could be progressive in his work. He understood that the spiritual and practical must work together for dreams to succeed, because that's the way God has made our world.

Sometimes we say, "God wants me to do this, so it *has* to work," because we don't want to actually *do* the work. Look at anyone who's successful, and behind the scenes there is a long, intense journey. That's even true of those who seem to be "overnight sensations." We want to rush or take shortcuts, then when our dream doesn't take off, we complain that God has disappointed us.

One of the basic principles in Scripture is that we reap what we sow (Gal. 6:7). If we sow poor business practices, then we will reap a failed company. If we skip the training we need, then we will not have the skills to be promoted when the time comes. If we sit back, then we will get left behind as our industry moves forward.

This doesn't mean striving. It simply means submitting to the ways God has made this world to work. Our God-sized dreams are a partnership with him. We do our part, and he does his. Our role is obedience and his is results.

We bring glory to God when we pursue our dreams not just with emotion but with excellence. Use your heart *and* your hands to serve him and others to the best of your ability.

Explore

Use a concordance or a site like www.crosswalk. com to do a keyword search for *work* in the book of Proverbs and see more practical wisdom about pursuing excellence.

Express

God, you are not just interested in the spiritual part of our God-sized dreams but in the practical as well. Please help me to be excellent in what I do so that it honors you and serves others well. When I'm tempted to skip the hard work or to hurry to the next thing, please give me the perseverance and persistence I need. Amen.

Experience

Let's get really practical with your God-sized dream today. What's one way you could grow that would enable you to be better at what you feel called to do? For example, you could read a book, sign up for a class, or find a mentor. Whatever that is, take the next step toward it today.

25

It's Okay for Your Dream to Be a Quiet One

Make it your ambition to lead a quiet life: You should mind your own business and work with your hands, just as we told you, so that your daily life may win the respect of outsiders and so that you will not be dependent on anybody.

1 Thessalonians 4:11-12

The latest scandal scrolls across the television screen. When the actress involved is asked how she feels about all the press, she shrugs her shoulders and says, "There's no such thing as bad publicity." Sure enough, her latest movie tops the charts the following week.

We live in a world where we consider loud to be good. Entertainment and getting attention are valued. How many eyeballs can we attract, clicks can we get, minutes of fame can we grasp?

And yet in the middle of the noise there's a whisper inviting us to a different kind of life, a different kind of dream. "Make it your ambition to lead a quiet life" is the countercultural invitation issued in the verses for today.

It's okay if your dream isn't loud.
It's okay if it doesn't get much attention.
It's okay if no one even knows you're doing it.

I've fallen into the trap of leading a "loud" life before. In my world, it wasn't so much about attention as it was about busyness. My schedule screamed at me because it was so full. And over time I realized I was hoping it would declare to everyone else, "Look how wanted she is!" My intense life came from a place of deep insecurity. I thought if I could just be busy enough, then I could prove that I was desired, valued, and loved.

During that season I would read the verses above and feel totally confused. It felt so different than my daily experience. Yet over time God showed me that I could let go of being so busy, and that even more importantly, I could only do so as I became quiet on the inside first.

> Being quiet on the inside means knowing we don't have to strive because we are already enough in Jesus.
>
> Being quiet on the inside means we don't have to prove our worth but rather we can receive it.
>
> Being quiet on the inside means living with a calm confidence that doesn't need to convince the world how much we matter.

So "living a quiet life" means two things: being willing to pursue our God-sized dream even if no one ever sees or knows it. And it means that even when our God-sized dream requires us to

Opening the Door to Your God-Sized Dream

be outwardly busy for a season, we let God teach our hearts to be at peace.

When we embrace those two aspects, it lets us settle down and do what comes next in the Scriptures above: "work with our hands." Like we talked about before, that means doing what's in front of us each day.

And when it comes to your God-sized dreams, you can find comfort in knowing you don't need a stage. You don't need a spotlight. You don't have to grab the attention of millions of people.

Your God-sized dream can happen quietly in what seems like a small way and still make a big difference.

Elijah the prophet knew all about making a big show. God used him to publicly stand up to the prophets of Baal. Yet when God revealed his presence to Elijah, he did it through a whisper. It was as if God knew Elijah needed to understand that while there is a time and place for loud, there is tremendous power in the quiet and hidden too.

In our loud world, God's presence is often revealed best through the "quietness" of our lives and hearts too.

Explore

Read the story of how God revealed himself to
Elijah through a whisper in 1 Kings 19:11–13.

Express

*God, thank you that you invite me to make it my
ambition to lead a quiet life. In a world that is
so loud, it's so reassuring to know I don't have to
shout to make a difference in your kingdom. If
there is static in my life or heart, please reveal it
to me and help me get rid of it so that my life and
heart can be quiet in the ways you intend. Amen.*

Experience

Ask yourself this really tough question: Would I
still pursue this God-sized dream even if no one
ever knew it was me doing it? If you felt some
hesitation in saying yes, then ask God to reveal
what part of you still needs to be validated and
receive that from him instead of your dream.

26

How to Cure Your Fear of the Future

She is clothed with strength and
dignity;
she can laugh at the days to come.

Proverbs 31:25

I catch a few moments of a news program featuring guests who are talking about the future. One predicts financial doom. Another shares a new medical condition that's sure to wreak havoc on lives. The next encourages viewers to stockpile because you never know when the next natural disaster may strike. By the time the show is done, I'm ready to hide in my closet and never come out.

Yes, I believe in being wise about the future as well as what's happening in our world. *But there is a difference between wisdom and fear.* That's especially important to note when it comes to our God-sized dreams.

So how do we live without fear of the future even as we pursue desires in our hearts that make our knees knock?

The ultimate God-sized dreams girl shows us how in the well-known Proverbs 31 chapter.

Here are a few of the God-sized dreams she pursued:

Being a wife of noble character

Real estate investing

Running a vineyard

Making a difference in the lives of the poor

Having a family who's respected in the community

Living a beautiful life

Building a profitable business

Gaining wisdom

Opening the Door to Your God-Sized Dream

Scripture tells us, "She sets about her work vigorously; her arms are strong for her tasks" (Prov. 31:17). This woman has a life full of verbs. She brings, selects, works, gets up, provides, considers, plants, sees, holds, grasps, extends, makes, sells, supplies, speaks, watches, and fears the Lord. While her virtues are often praised, it's clear that all of them are more than simply beliefs. She's a woman of action. Even in the small things, she's always taking the next step.

And when you are always taking the next step of obedience, fear of the future diminishes.

The only way to cure fear of the future is to be faithful with what's been entrusted to you today—and to actually do it. Most of our fears are based on fantasy, "What if I release this book and no one wants it?" "What if I go to that get-together to build relationships and no one wants to talk to me?" "What if I take this next step and it doesn't work out the way I want?" As long as we stay in that stage, fear can reign because there's no reality to conflict with our perception of what will happen.

Faith trumps fear not by simply wishing it away but by action. Many times when God says to his people, "Do not fear," it is followed by some kind of specific instruction. He's reassuring them and then showing them what they will need to do to replace that fear with faith.

In the life of the Proverbs 31 woman, we see this in two specific ways: strength and dignity. She is "clothed with strength and dignity"; therefore, she can laugh at the days to come.

Strength conveys that she's willing to do whatever it takes to see God's purposes for her life fulfilled. She doesn't just talk the talk, she walks the walk.

Dignity describes her character—how she conducts herself as she takes action.

Doing what you need to do right now and becoming who God wants you to be a little more each day are the two best ways to face the future without fear. Your God-sized dreams will require both of those aspects.

I imagine the future trying to taunt the Proverbs 31 woman by telling her that she doesn't have what it takes, that God's plans for her will never unfold, that she is getting older by the minute. Her response? Laughter. "You silly future," she might say, "I'm too busy to worry about you. I'm living what God has for me today—and I will do the same tomorrow too."

We can join her as women who are confident our future is in God's hands. And that means we can focus on what he has for our hands to do right here and now.

Explore

Read more about our God-sized dreams sister in Proverbs 31:10–31.

Express

God, I'm so glad I don't have to be afraid of the future because of you. When I'm tempted to get caught up in questions of "What if?" help me to refocus on what you have asked me to do today. Thank you for giving me the strength I need for my tasks and for enabling me to face what's to come with joy, not dread. Amen.

Experience

One quality the Proverbs 31 woman displayed in every area of her life was being intentional. She lived a proactive rather than reactive life. How are you intentional about your day—do you use a calendar, a sticky note, a journal, or some other way to take time to plan and prepare with God? Sometimes we stop at "having a quiet time," but God wants to be involved in the practical aspects of our lives as well. Pause for a few moments and pray through your entire day with him, asking for wisdom in each task you need to complete.

Opening the Door to Your God-Sized Dream

27

Go Ahead and Let Your Light Shine

Let your light shine before others, that they may see your good deeds and glorify your Father in heaven.

Matthew 5:16

We've snatched a quiet corner in the middle of a noisy get-together. She's telling me exciting news—someone wants her to come and speak. It's a God-sized dream come true. She chatters excitely about the details and then pauses. Her eyes drift to the ground as she whispers, "But I don't want it to be about me."

Our God-sized dreams can cause us to feel deeply conflicted. On one hand, we sense a desire within us that draws us forward. On the other hand, we fear somehow we might steal the spotlight from God, so we try to shrink back into the shadows to make sure that doesn't happen.

So what do we do? First of all, if you're even asking yourself those questions and trying to avoid making it about you, then your heart is most likely in the right place. But let's talk more specifically about what that means so you can dismiss those worries and get on with your dream.

In the gospel of Matthew, Jesus shares with the people how they are to live. Consider these two passages:

> You are the light of the world. A town built on a hill cannot be hidden. Neither do people light a lamp and put it under a bowl. Instead they put it on its stand, and it gives light to everyone in the house. In the same way, let your light shine before others, that they may

see your good deeds and glorify your Father in heaven. (Matt. 5:14–16)

Be careful not to practice your righteousness in front of others to be seen by them. If you do, you will have no reward from your Father in heaven. . . . But when you give to the needy, do not let your left hand know what your right hand is doing, so that your giving may be in secret. Then your Father, who sees what is done in secret, will reward you. (Matt. 6:1, 3–4)

Jesus goes on to share more things, like prayer, that we're to keep private as well. I used to read those two passages and walk away completely confused. (I hope I'm not the only one who ever feels that way after reading the Bible.) Jesus seemed to be saying two different things—shine and hide.

So on the journey to my God-sized dreams, I found myself alternating between the two. I'd step boldly into the calling God had for my life, but as soon as I got any attention at all I'd retreat.

Yet over time I came to see what Jesus really meant. The secret is to recognize we're not to "practice *our righteousness* in front of others." In other words, the Pharisees were living to show the world, "Look what a good person I am." While Jesus said we're the light of the world, and that means living in a way that shows the world, "Look how good God is."

It all comes down to motivation. What is the *source* of our light, and what do we want the result of our shining to be? If we believe that we are good people who deserve the praise of others, then we're falling into the Pharisee camp. If we believe that we are sinners who have been miraculously transformed by Christ and now have his life within them to share with the world, then we are shining as intended.

Here's the tricky part: you can't always tell the difference from the outside. Two women can stand on the exact same stage and one can be shining while the other is showing off. What distinguishes the two is the condition of their hearts.

So how do you make sure you're being a light in the way God intends? Simply say to him, "God,

Opening the Door to Your God-Sized Dream

I acknowledge that you are the source of the light in me. I want to shine so that others can see you in and through me. I humbly ask you to use me for your purposes. If there is any motivation in my heart that needs to change, I give you full freedom to reveal it to me and help me change it. In the meantime, I'm moving forward with you in this dream."

That's it.

And it's okay for you to receive joy, fulfillment, and the many other benefits that God has for you when you live out his purpose for your life. That is not selfish—that's the way he intended it to work.

The enemy will try to accuse you of doing things for selfish motives, of taking attention from Jesus, of all sorts of things. When that happens, just do a quick heart check with Jesus and then keep on shining. As long as you are aware of that struggle, it means that you are winning it.

Go ahead and shine, girl. We need that light that's within you. And no one can brighten this world quite like you.

Explore

Read more about when to shine and what to keep hidden in Matthew 6:1–23.

Express

God, I want to shine for you. My human nature sometimes tries to interfere with that either by shrinking back into the shadows or by trying to grab the spotlight. My true desire is to do neither but instead to let you use me in whatever way you want. If that means getting attention from others, so be it. If that means doing all I do in secret, so be it. I'm your servant and you can use me to shine in whatever way you want. Amen.

Experience

Go into a dark room and turn on a lamp. Think for a few minutes about what it means to be a light in a dark world. What new insights does God have to reveal to your heart?

Opening the Door to Your God-Sized Dream

28

Keep Your Focus

*But one thing I do: Forgetting what is
behind and straining toward what is
ahead, I press on toward the goal to win
the prize for which God has called me
heavenward in Christ Jesus.*

Philippians 3:13–14

I curl the covers around me and press my head
deeper into the pillow. But sleep won't come.
Every time I close my eyes all I can see is my
calendar staring back at me. It's filled to overflow-
ing. I find myself longing to shred it and run away

to a remote island. "What's the matter with me, God?" I whisper. "That calendar is full of *good* things. So why am I exhausted?"

God used that low point to gently begin showing me the difference between what's good and what's truly best in my life. For years I had misinterpreted a Scripture we all know well: "I can do all things through Christ who strengthens me" (Phil. 4:13 NKJV). When I read those words this was my translation: *I have to do it all* through Christ who strengthens me.

Then another phrase by the apostle Paul in the very same book caught my heart one day. Exactly one chapter before the Scripture above he says, "But this one thing I do" (Phil. 3:13 NRSV). He goes on to share how he is pressing on toward the goal God has for him.

The contrast between those two verses bounced around in my mind for days. Here's what it means: we are capable of doing all things through Christ, but we are only called to do specifically what he asks of us. Just because something is "good" doesn't mean it's his will for your life.

As dreamers and visionaries, we can find this

Opening the Door to Your God-Sized Dream

to be even more of a struggle. I realized this one day when some friends gently pointed out a truth I needed to hear. Over dessert at our favorite lunch spot, I shared how weary I felt and how hard it was for me to rest. "I never feel like what I do is enough," I confessed between bites of chocolate cake.

I will never forget what my wise friend said next. She looked me in the eyes and said, "Holley, you're a dreamer. You will always be able to think up more than you can actually do. And God doesn't expect you to do it all." My other friends around the table nodded in agreement.

I set my spoon down with a smile. They were so right! I felt guilt replaced by peace as I understood that rather than following every idea that came into my mind, I could truly focus on what God asked of me.

That leads to the question: How do we know what God wants us to do? Romans 12:2 offers us three steps: "Do not conform to the pattern of this world, but be transformed by the renewing of your mind. Then you will be able to test and approve what God's will is—his good, pleasing and perfect will."

First, we are to recognize that God's ways are different than those of the world around us. We live in a culture that will always drive us to be busy and exhausted. We have to hit the pause button and decide to live differently.

Then we need to identify the lies we're believing (like I was) and replace them with the truth so that our hearts are free to choose God's best rather than reacting in fear or guilt.

Finally, we've got to "test and approve God's will." In other words, we take action and when we realize we need to change the way we're living, we do.

You are free to focus on your God-sized dream. Actually, doing so is the only way it can actually happen.

You don't have to do it all.

You simply have to answer God's call.

Explore

Read Philippians 3:7–14 and 4:8–13.

Opening the Door to Your God-Sized Dream

Express

God, you made me a dreamer, and that means so many plans and ideas come into my mind. I love to say yes and be part of new adventures. Yet I realize sometimes that can distract me from what's truly best in my life. I pray you will give me the wisdom, discernment, and self-control I need to focus on your will for my life. Amen.

Experience

Make a list of all the commitments in your life right now. Are there any that it's time to let go of so you can focus more on your God-sized dream?

29

Be Who You Want to Be Around

But encourage one another daily, as long as it is called "Today," so that none of you may be hardened by sin's deceitfulness.

Hebrews 3:13

If you haven't noticed yet, I work in coffee shops a lot. And there's one thing you can't help doing in a coffee shop (besides getting your share of caffeine) and that's eavesdropping. Over time you hear a lot about families, businesses, and even faith. The biggest surprise? Most of the conversations I overhear are negative. Whether it's the weather or the latest family drama, everyone has a complaint or criticism to share.

This phenomenon is nothing new. All the way back in the Old Testament the Israelites got in trouble for "grumbling" in the desert rather than trusting in God. And it's no coincidence that they did so in a group. Researcher Daniel Goleman explains that we catch each other's moods in much the same way that we catch colds. Our brains are so wired to be relational that we can't help but be affected by those around us.[1]

If you're like me, that makes you want to sit back and say, "See? If those negative people could get their act together, then I could be a lot more joyful!" But the truth is we're responsible for our words and attitudes. And there's good news: one positive person can uplift a whole group.

Understanding this especially matters for those of us who are God-sized dreamers because we simply can't afford the time, energy, and emotion to be negative. It's up to us to be committed to shifting conversations and encouraging those around us. In other words . . .

Be who you want to be around.

Because over time you will influence those around you.

So if you find yourself in the middle of gossip or a gripe fest, what can you do?

Here's my go-to list of three kinds of questions to ask to help the conversation get back on track. (If you're the one doing the gossiping and griping, ask *yourself* these questions. Ha!)

If you find yourself stuck in a negative conversation, ask a question that's

Personal—e.g.: What do you think will help? (Use when someone is saying, "The whole world/office/family is a mess.")

Positive—e.g.: What's going well in the middle of all of that? (Use when someone is saying, "Here are the ten reasons why the whole world/office/family is a mess.")

Pointed—e.g.: What's a small step you could take? (Use when someone is saying, "And if everyone else would just get their act

Opening the Door to Your God-Sized Dream

together, the world/office/family would no longer be a mess.")

And, yes, the world/office/family is likely to be a mess—probably always has been, always will be. So while negative talk makes it feel like we're doing something about that, we're actually just wasting valuable time, words, and energy that could be used for encouraging others and acting on solutions (the little bit we really can do) instead.

The best part? Research has also shown that those who have a bright outlook on life tend to have stronger relationships, better health, more success, and even longer lives. Not only do we benefit from having a positive attitude, but we can also help others experience more success.

The world is always going to find something to complain about because that's simply part of human nature. But you can be different. I can be different. And when we are, our relationships become different too.

God-sized dreams never happen alone. Be who you want to be around on the way to your dreams, and the journey will be better for everyone.

Be Who You Want to Be Around

Explore

Read Hebrews 3:7–19 to see why encouraging each other is so important, especially on the way to our God-sized dreams.

Express

God, you know this world can be so negative. Instead of giving in to that, I pray you will help me be someone who lives and speaks with courage, faith, and joy. Use me to encourage those I connect with today and to be the kind of person I want to be around. Amen.

Experience

Carry a little piece of paper around with you for one day and make a mark on it every time you hear or say something encouraging.

30

How You Can Handle the Ups and Downs

Suppose one of you wants to build a tower. Won't you first sit down and estimate the cost to see if you have enough money to complete it?

Luke 14:28

The sun has barely slipped over the hills in the distance as we gather at the starting line. I'm at a fifty-mile bike ride and already questioning what in the world I'm doing here instead of still being in bed. My husband looks at me and says, "You'll be fine." I'm not convinced. I cast a concerned look at my friend who's riding with me. "I'll take care of you," she says. I take a deep breath. My husband has promised there will be free cookies every ten miles at the break stations. I try to fixate on this bit of hope. I also think of the other advice he gives me before every ride: "Plan for the hills. Try to keep a steady pace. Don't use up all your energy at the beginning."

Before I know it we're on our way. When I want to speed up, I intentionally stay at a slower pace. When I see a hill coming, I build momentum and shift my gears. Click-click-click. I've learned to be strategic about how I climb. And as I buzz past other bikers I can't help but smile. It actually worked.

As I cross the finish line, I'm tired but not exhausted. I grab a bottle of water and a hot dog, then hold both high in the air in a declaration of victory. I made it. As I sit on the curb to rest, I reflect back on how far I've come. I used to completely wear myself out about halfway through the ride. I never planned for the ups and downs. Doing so has made all the difference.

It's the same way in the rest of my life too. When I had a God-sized dream to pursue, I'd take off at full speed only to find myself exhausted. My husband calls the cure for this "planning for the hills," while Jesus has another name for it—"counting the cost." Really they both mean the same thing—consider what it's going to take and prepare for it.

God-sized dreams are a lot like a bike ride. There are many ups and downs, times of intense pedaling and times when it feels like you're coasting. What matters most is learning to plan for both. What do you need to cross the finish line of your dream well?

As I write this, I'm just coming over the top of a hill in my life. A particularly busy month, a book launch, and an upcoming deadline meant I had to give words my all for a season. Today I could finally take a deep breath (and a nap). I also took a few minutes to make a list of what helps me get over the "hills" in my journey so I can refer to it in the future.

Here are a few things that made my list:

Naps

Baths

Dates with my husband
Time to think and pray
Having a clean house
Sticking to my exercise schedule
Reading

I shared this with two friends and they said, "What about pedicures?" I laughed and replied, "No way! No one touches my feet." They thought I was nuts. But, hey, no two bikers climb hills the same and no two people approach the intense time of their God-sized dreams the same way either. You'll notice my list isn't super "spiritual." I believe God made us spiritual, physical, emotional, and social beings. So we've got to consider what we need in all of those areas. We can be praying day and night, but if we're eating poorly and not getting rest, then we're going to be compromised in our ability to pursue God's best for us.

Also, it's important to give ourselves permission to coast. That's the best part of the backside of a hill when you ride—you get to enjoy the benefits of the climb you just did by not needing to pedal quite so hard for a bit.

We talked before about how dreamers can always think of more to do. But at some point we have to say, "I've done what God asked me to do and now it's time to rest." You can't go full speed on your bike or in your life all the time. Doing so is asking for burnout before you cross the finish line.

God-sized dreams are long-term commitments. They're a fifty-mile ride, not a short sprint around the block. You will have many ups and downs along the way. By planning and preparing for both, you can cross the finish line with a smile.

And remember to stop for a few cookies along the way.

Explore

Read Luke 14:25–33 to see the steep hills that are part of being a disciple (another word for a God-sized dreamer).

Express

God, it's easy to get excited about what's ahead without pausing to consider what it really requires. I pray that you will give me wisdom to plan and prepare so that I have what I need to finish what you have asked me to start. Help me to know when to pedal harder and when to rest. I want to keep pace with you. Amen.

Experience

Draw the ups and downs of your God-sized dream so far. What has helped you in the really intense times? What has helped you in the more restful ones?

31

What to Do When the Lies Get Loud

Then you will know the truth, and the truth will set you free.

John 8:32

"You're selfish for pursuing this God-sized dream."

"You're going to fail and everyone is going to know it."

"You don't have anything big enough to offer."

If you're pursuing a God-sized dream, expect the lies to come. In the Garden of Eden the enemy deceived Eve with one question, "Did God really say?" and he has thrown untruth at our hearts ever since. When you dare to take a step forward for the kingdom, you put yourself on the front lines of the battle for truth.

The lies wound us, and then we feel ashamed. We assume we must be doing something wrong. After all, aren't all our sisters having victory? But this is universal: if you are a God-sized dreamer, you will have to battle lies. The particular one that comes at you will be unique to you, but we all must deal with them.

Thankfully, we do have what we need to combat those attacks. In the passage Paul wrote about the armor of God, he says, "Take up the shield of faith, with which you can extinguish all the flaming arrows of the evil one" (Eph. 6:16). This means holding on to what we know is true no matter what lies the enemy or our flesh may try to tell us.

Jesus said, "If you hold to my teaching, you are really my disciples. Then you will know the truth, and the truth will set you free" (John 8:31–32). Did you catch the order in those verses? First we hold on to truth, *then* we know it, and *then* we are set free.

We expect that the moment we intellectually receive a truth it will become real in every part of our lives. Then we experience guilt or shame when that's not the case. But that isn't how it works. First we're to hold on to truth even in the heat of battle and then we truly know it deep down in our hearts because we've experienced it—and that's when it sets us free.

You are not alone in the lies you have to battle. And we can't do this on our own. We need others to hold up the shield of faith for us sometimes too. Just this week I had a thought that refused to go away. I knew it wasn't true, but I couldn't shake it. I sent an email to my life coach, Denise Martin, and said, "This is the lie I'm hearing. I know it isn't true, but I'm stuck and I don't know what truth to replace it with instead." I also told God, "I have no idea what to do about this. I need some insight because I'm losing this battle." Through that vulnerability and relationship, God gave me what I needed. Years ago I wouldn't have done the same thing. Instead I would have said, "I need to have it all together. I'm not supposed to struggle or feel weak." But when we tell ourselves that, we leave our hearts unguarded and get wounded by the enemy.

There is no shame in asking for help, especially when we're struggling to overcome the lies in our lives.

Close your eyes for a moment and listen to your heart.

Do you hear the lies?

Now listen again for the truth calling to you—inviting you into freedom and the joy of a God-sized dream that's so much more real than anything you feel.

Explore
....

Read about the other pieces of armor available to you in Ephesians 6:10–17.

Express
....

God, you are full of grace and truth. I want your voice to be the loudest in my life and heart. Where I'm hearing lies, please show me what you want to speak to me instead. Please send people who love me into my life who will remind me of the truth I need to hold on to as well. Amen.

Experience

We all have a "signature lie" that we hear more often than any other when it comes to our God-sized dream. What's yours? And what's the truth God wants to replace it with? If you're not sure, ask someone you trust to help you figure it out.

32

When You Really Want
to Change the World

*Therefore go and make disciples of all
nations, baptizing them in the name
of the Father and of the Son and of
the Holy Spirit, and teaching them to
obey everything I have commanded
you. And surely I am with you always,
to the very end of the age.*

Matthew 28:19–20

Genny Heika's words leap off the page at me and
grab hold of my heart: "God has been shaping

me these past several years—patiently steering me away from my ideas of what my life should look like, and growing the passions in my heart to lead me to what I'm supposed to be doing."[1]

I find myself nodding and smiling as she shares how she began with very specific plans for what her God-sized dreams would look like. And then God led her to broaden all those ideas to simply this: *help change the world.*

I can relate because my journey has been much the same. And as I've talked to other God-sized dreamers, I've heard similar scenarios. Our agendas gradually give way to God's true purposes for our lives.

That's why I'm passionate about seeing women pursue God-sized dreams. It's not because I believe they will get what they think they want. Instead it's because when we choose to open the door to what God has for us, then we can get what we really need—and that is more of him in our lives. In many ways, God-sized dreams are interchangeable. It's the process that matters. It's really about where we go with Jesus and how he takes hold of our hearts along the way.

At the bottom of Genny's post, I left a comment telling her how much I loved what she shared. At the end I added, "Funny how when we want to change the world, the first thing God changes is our hearts."

We tend to think of God-sized dreams as external—events, accomplishments, or shifts in the direction of our lives. But I've come to believe that the most important parts are internal—how our hearts change, who we become, the ways God transforms our perspective on life.

We see this with Jesus and the disciples. They all had expectations of what their God-sized dream (the Messiah) would be and what they would receive for following him. Jesus turned all of this upside down. He spent three years with them making sure their hearts were changed to align with his, and then he sent them out to help others do the same—to change the world.

So even if you're not sure what your dream is or if it seems to be changing shape along the way, keep pressing forward.

In many ways, being a God-sized dreamer is about an attitude first and then about the specific action. When you choose to dream you are saying yes to God's work in your life, and he will surprise you again and again about what that really means.

As Genny says:

> I've seen how God uses our dreams—the desires he plants in our hearts from the very beginning—even dreams like mine of writing and encouraging others—to change lives. Not necessarily in the way we imagined. And not necessarily in the timeframe we hoped for. But he uses them, and he grows them, and his dreams are bigger than ours could ever be.[2]

And the biggest change of all is the one that takes place within us. When that happens, it spills over into our lives and around us until the world really does change too.

Explore

Read Matthew 28, where the disciples experience a God-sized dream come true (the resurrection) and then are sent out by Jesus.

Express

God, no matter what may be in my heart or mind regarding God-sized dreams, I know ultimately you are asking me to change the world for your kingdom. Please show me how you would like for me to do so. I release my ideas to you and open my heart up to the mystery of who you are and how you work. Amen.

Experience

Think back to a dream you had earlier in your life, perhaps even in your childhood. How did it turn out differently than what you expected? How did you change along the way too?

33

What Every God-Sized Dream Ultimately Points Our Hearts To

My beloved is mine and I am his.

Song of Songs 2:16

I'm sitting on the back deck of a restaurant over-looking the ocean. Orange and scarlet clouds drift toward the waves as music plays in the background. I close my eyes and in that most beautiful of places, that happiest of moments, my heart also feels an ache—a longing I can't quite name.

Have you ever felt the same?

God-sized dreams make me feel that way too.

They make the veil between heaven and earth feel thinner until it seems we can almost touch the other side.

That's what every God-sized dream ultimately points our hearts to:

Home.
Beyond this world.
Past the suffering.
Into the glory.

Jennifer Camp says:

You know how that heart of yours aches for something to grasp a hold of? How it yearns for discovery of identity, claiming of passion, awakening to adventure? You spend a lot of your life trying to figure out who you are. You look for people—community, family, friends—to live life with. You gradually, on a time-table all your own, grow in courage and willingness to heed those whispers in your heart from that God of yours who loves you, who adores you, who waits for you with joy and excitement, who calls you his own.

You have within you a dream placed on your heart by God—a dream perfectly sized and created just for you to step into. It is the beginning of you, the start of you seeing God more fully, the opportunity for you to experience God more completely.[1]

We long to be settled where we are, and yet I believe we're made to live with a bit of longing. I call it "divine discontent." It's a restlessness within us that whispers, "You're not home yet."

At its best, that longing leads us closer to Jesus. Those aching-happy moments point us to the incompleteness of who we are, of how we live—how even at its very best this life is not enough to fully satisfy us.

Your truest God-sized dream will not happen until you step from this life to the next. Every dream until then is just a preview, a shadow of the glory of the One who places those dreams in your heart.

What does this mean? Seek to see him in your God-sized dreams. And realize that even the best, most beautiful dream can't take his place. Not even if it comes true beyond your wildest imagination. There will always be a part of you that longs for something *more*.

Rather than resisting this or feeling guilty about it, embrace it. See it for what it is: the wooing of your heart by the One who wants it for all eternity.

He is the longing you can't name, the desire you can't satisfy, the whisper in those beautiful moments that dares you to believe "the best is yet to be."

Because the best really is yet to be.

For you.

For me.

Forever.

Explore

The Song of Songs is about love and longing. Many scholars view it as an analogy of the relationship between Christ and his bride, the church. Read Song of Songs 2 in this light.

Opening the Door to Your God-Sized Dream

Express

God, sometimes my heart aches to be home with you. Thank you for those moments when I long for more than this life. Help me to use them as reminders of what really matters and opportunities to draw closer to you. You are my ultimate dream come true. Amen.

Experience

Think back to the happiest or most beautiful moment you've experienced recently—the kind that makes your heart fill with longing. Where were you? What were you doing? What could God have been revealing to you in that moment?

34

What If Someone Else Is Already Living Your Dream?

What has been will be again,
what has been done will be done
again;
there is nothing new under the sun.

Ecclesiastes 1:9

I can almost hear the breathlessness in her email as she types, "Please don't share this with anyone. If it gets out, someone else might do it."

Later in the day a woman confesses, "There are already so many people doing what I feel called to do. How can my voice even make a difference?"

Then over dinner a friend says to me, "Even when I make progress, there's still someone doing it better than I am. Shouldn't I just cheer them on?"

I nod in understanding at the fear, questioning, and hesitation in these statements. When a God-sized dream first comes to us it often feels like a brand-new revelation—as if no one else in the whole history of the universe has ever thought of this idea. Then quickly we realize that whatever we want to do or share has already been done or said before. So we sigh and think, "Time to start over."

But that's the reality of God-sized dreams. Wise Solomon said, "There is *nothing new* under the sun." But he didn't say, "There is *no one new* under the sun." Because every one of us is one of a kind, and there will never be anyone else like us again. It doesn't matter if someone else has said it or done it already. *You haven't.* We need your version, your perspective, your voice in this world. You're simply irreplaceable.

And you are here for such a time as this—to share this God-sized dream with your generation.

I love how Scripture says, "David . . . served God's purpose in his own generation" (Acts 13:36). You are called to offer what God has placed within you to our world right here, right now. No one else will live the exact amount of time you will, in the place you will, with the people whom God will have cross your path.

You can't say, "Oh, they'll get what they need from someone else," because if God intends them to receive it through you, that's not true. "We are God's handiwork, created in Christ Jesus to do good works, which God prepared in advance for us to do" (Eph. 2:10). In other words, there are things in this world that only you can do. That means that there is no such thing as better in the kingdom—only different. You are not competing with your brothers and sisters. Instead all of us are *completing* God's plan together.

Lisa-Jo Baker says it this way:

No one can steal your dream because God has built it into you.

No one can write your book or design your art.

No one can launch your venture like you.

No one can do that secret impossible that you've got your heart set on instead of you.

You are the DNA of the dream.

Even if you both started with the exact same premise you'd end up glorious worlds apart as distinct as your fingerprints.

Because you are.

What God gives you he gives you on purpose.[1]

We need your part. We need your heart. We need *your* God-sized dream.

Explore

Read Ephesians 2 to see the calling we all share and yet each express differently.

Express

God, thank you for preparing good works in advance for me to do. When I'm tempted to compare myself to someone else, please help me refocus

*on you and who you've called me to be. I'm made
in your image, and there's a part of who you are
that you want to express through who I am. That's
a beautiful mystery. Amen.*

Experience

....

Make a small display in your home of objects that
are similar but different (e.g.: fruit or flowers) to
remind you of how we all have our own place and
purpose, but we're better together.

35

You've Already Come Farther Than You Realize

Jesus Christ is the same yesterday and today and forever.

Hebrews 13:8

Giggles erupt from the couch in my living room. I poke my head around the corner of the kitchen and ask, "What's so funny?"

One of my dearest friends points to a picture of me from junior high in a scrapbook she's managed to find. "Look at your bangs!" she gleefully declares.

"Like yours were so much better," I tease back.

"I know," she says. "What were we thinking?" We dive into a discussion of all the fashion mistakes we wish we could take back. By the end we've laughed so hard our sides hurt. I look down at my outfit for the day—the one I was so unsure of this morning—and suddenly I realize my accessorizing skills have come a lot farther than I realized.

That's how it goes with progress. We often don't even know it's happening. It usually takes someone else pointing it out or an intentional look-back to realize that, wow, we're sure not where we used to be.

When we're on the journey to a God-sized dream, it often works the same way. We're so focused on the future. Each new thing causes us to feel fear and we wonder, "Can I do this?" And it becomes easy to overlook how much we've already done.

All the way back to ancient Israel, God gave his people a strategy for dealing with this tendency in human nature. He asked the Israelites to set up physical markers to remind them of how far they'd come with him. Like that photo

Opening the Door to Your God-Sized Dream

in my scrapbook, those markers became tangible symbols that said, "You can keep moving forward because you already know God is faithful and that if you are obedient to him, there's nothing that can keep you from all he has for your life."

What are you facing today? Think back to another time when you faced something you didn't think you could get through either. Yet here you are. What helped you? Perhaps you leaned on trusted friends, spent extra time in God's Word, or dared to take a risk and learned something in the process. While the circumstances might be different, what helped you then applies now too. What you're facing probably feels totally new, but chances are you already have tools and strengths to get through it.

And, most of all, even when our circumstances change, we can rest in knowing that "Jesus Christ is the same yesterday and today and forever" (Heb. 13:8). The God who loved me with big bangs in junior high still loves me in skinny jeans today (hmm, I may regret those one day too).

When your God-sized dream begins to feel overwhelming, use your past to push you forward.

You've Already Come Farther Than You Realize

Look back and intentionally see how far you've come and how God has been with you every step of the way.

He still is today.

And you're wiser, stronger, and braver than you've ever been before.

Explore

Read about how Jacob set up an altar to help him remember what God had done for him in Genesis 35:1–14.

Express

God, I love exploring the future with you, and yet I know sometimes I need to pause to look back too. Thank you for your faithfulness to me all my life. There has never been anything I haven't been able to get through with you—and there never will be. You're growing me each day, and I know you will make sure I have all I need to complete your purpose for my life.

Experience

Write down a time when God helped you to step into something new or got you through a difficult time. What helped you then that you can apply now?

36

When Your Heart Needs
Some Encouragement

*But David encouraged himself in the
Lord his God.*

1 Samuel 30:6 KJV

I'm chatting with a couple of wise friends on the
phone. They ask me what I'm struggling with
most at this point in my journey. I think for a
moment and then respond, "I just want someone
to tell me every day that I'm doing a good job,
that I'm on the right track." I share how when
I worked at a corporate job I had an amazing

boss who would give me feedback and affirm I was heading in a positive direction. Sometimes I really miss that voice in my life.

When you're a God-sized dreamer, one of the hardest parts is that you're trailblazing in the kingdom. That means there often isn't anyone to say, "I've been exactly where you are—keep at it." Yes, we are to find others to encourage us. And we're to have mentors and peers who can offer wisdom and insight because they've gone through similar things. But there will come a time when you've heard the truth God wants to whisper to your heart, others have spoken into your life, and it's time for one more person on the list to encourage you too: and that's you.

It can sound odd to talk about encouraging yourself—it can even feel arrogant. But we're not talking about bragging or smiling in the mirror and saying, "Hey, you're something really special." What encouraging ourselves means is reminding our hearts of what we already know to be true.

David "encouraged himself in the Lord his God" after facing an incredibly difficult situation.

Even those closest to him were too upset to help him out. He had to bring to mind what he knew about God and what his faith could enable him to do. As a result, he led the people to a great victory.

I don't know about you, but I'm my own worst critic. I can encourage other women all day long, but I wrestle with having a different standard for myself. Michele-Lyn shares a similar struggle on her blog, *A Life Surrendered*:

> Do you ever wake up in the morning and it seems like a rogue wave of discouragement was waiting for you so it can knock you down? A wave of discouragement that sweeps you off your feet and shrouds you in darkness that presses in all around before you ever saw it coming? In confusion, you try to get back to your feet, and wonder what hit you?
>
> You try and catch your bearing, and the lies pummel, before you have a chance to make them out from the truth.
>
> I raise my hand to say, "Yes, I've been battling this heaviness and these lies . . ."

"You're wasting your time."

"No one's going to get it."

"You've disappointed them."

"You think they want to read about your junk?"

"Who do you think you are?"

And then question, "What am I even doing here in the first place?"

I have a choice to make. We all do in this place.

We run and hide and give up, or we can encourage our own soul.[1]

When I read Michele-Lyn's words I wanted to stand up and cheer because I felt like someone else understood the battle I faced within. And I imagine you do too.

On the journey to our God-sized dreams, we will have many people by our side who will help get us through. Yet there is one person who must be on your side too—and that's you.

When you choose to be on your own side, then you are standing with God because *he is for you*. He has told you what is true, and it's okay to remind yourself of that as often as you need to, especially as you pursue your God-sized dream.

We're called to be encouragers to those around us.

And to the heart within us too.

Explore

Read about how David saw a God-sized dream come true after he encouraged himself in the Lord in 1 Samuel 30:1–19.

Express

God, it can seem much easier to encourage others than to do the same with my own heart. Thank you for the truth you've spoken to me about who I am and what you've called me to do. Help me to remind myself of what's true, especially when I feel alone. You are on my side and so I want to be too. Amen.

Opening the Door to Your God-Sized Dream

Experience

....

What is one truth that you need to be reminded of each day right now? Write it on a notecard along with a Scripture that goes with it and put it in a place you'll see.

37

Your Dreams
Do Not Define You

*See what great love the Father has
lavished on us, that we should be called
children of God! And that is what we are!*

1 John 3:1

"I want to be a speaker."
"I want to be a mom."
"I want to be a CEO."

When we think of our God-sized dreams, they
often involve roles that we believe will define

us. Somewhere deep inside us is a voice that whispers, "You won't really be anything until you're a ..."

Having something define us makes us feel more secure. It seems like it will soothe the questions and doubts within us. Yet the more dreamers I talk to, the more I see this is actually what's true: *a God-sized dream is more likely to refine you than define you.*

Here's what I mean. We start off on the journey with the idea that if only we can achieve our dream, then we will finally know who we really are and have what we really want in life. But God has his own agenda. You see, he's already told us who we are.

> Chosen.
> Loved.
> Wonderfully made.

(Just to name a few.)

And he's committed to us hanging on to who he says we are because he knows it's the only source of true security. Everything else can be changed.

Your Dreams Do Not Define You

Jesus told a parable about two men who decided to build houses. One built his house upon a rock. The other built his upon sand. When life's storms came, guess which house was still standing?

God loves us too much to let us build our lives on foundations like "author" or "wife" or "ministry leader." He will never let you define yourself by your God-sized dream.

I see this unfold in two ways. The first is when a God-sized dream doesn't come true. Through disappointment a dreamer comes to see that what she really wanted isn't going to happen. She reevaluates her life and discovers that she's already enough because of who she is in Christ and that God has even better plans for her than she did for herself.

The other scenario is when a God-sized dream does come true. It's often then that a woman realizes, "I thought this would fulfill me and change the way I see myself, but it hasn't." She becomes disillusioned with the dream for a season until it takes the proper place in her life—as a way she serves God with the gifts she's been given.

I've experienced both of the above with different dreams. Neither one are much fun at the time. But they also lead to tremendous freedom. Because as much as we may think we want to be defined, our hearts were really made to be free.

One day we realize the definition we thought would make us secure is really more like a prison cell that restricts us. It's in that moment that Jesus stands before us with the key and says, "Come out, daughter, I have so much more for you. You don't need this place to feel safe. Instead you can have true security in me."

When we step out of what we think our God-sized dream has to be and instead let God make it whatever he wants, we begin to change. Rather than being defined, we're refined in ways that make us more like Jesus and lead us into his best for our lives (which is beyond what we can even dream).

That's what opening the door to all God has for you really means. And there's so much for you on the other side.

Explore

One reason we can try to define ourselves through our dreams is because we're not sure who God really says we are. If you do an internet search for "our identity in Christ," many different lists that share verses on that topic will pop up.

Express

God, it amazes me that you say I'm loved, chosen, cherished, and more. You speak to the deepest places of my heart. Help me to hear your voice and cling to what you say is true about me. When I try to place my security in things that can never really be depended upon, bring me back to the foundation you've already given me. Amen.

Experience

What is the definition that goes with your God-sized dream (e.g.: speaker, mom, CEO)? Take a moment to write that down and release it to God (yep, this will scare you silly).

38

When It's Time
to Pass Your Dream On
to Someone New

*But the plans of the LORD stand firm
   forever,
   the purposes of his heart through
   all generations.*

Psalm 33:11

The commercial shares about a site where you can explore your family tree for generations. A man declares, "I never knew my great-grandfather was in my profession too!" A woman exclaims, "I come from a long line of great cooks." Time has a way of eclipsing our past. We can forget that much of who we are today can be tied back to many generations before us.

The same is true for our God-sized dreams. When they come into our lives, they feel as if they are brand-new. And they are to us. But whatever dream you're pursuing now also has a long history in God's kingdom. That's because the creative ways God finds to reach people in each generation change, but the purposes of his heart (like the verse above talks about) remain the same.

In my life, I can literally trace my God-sized dream back through the limbs of my family tree. My grandparents owned a Christian bookstore. Their God-sized dream was to spread the message of Jesus in their generation. Through their faith and example, they helped make it possible for me to pursue that same dream in a different way many years later.

Another friend of mine has a completely different story. She grew up in a family that didn't believe. But one day in college a woman shared

Opening the Door to Your God-Sized Dream

Jesus with her through a campus ministry. My friend became a Christian, and now she does the same for other college students. Looking at the family tree of her dream would take you all the way back to the founder of that campus ministry (and even beyond).

Especially in our individualistic culture, it can seem as if our God-sized dreams are independent of the past and other people. But neither are true. You are part of a purpose in God's heart that he's committed to expressing in every generation. I believe that's one reason for all those long genealogies in the Bible! We need to be reminded of who has come before us.

And that means this is also true: you will be called to pass your dream on to someone else too. The experiences you're gaining, what you're learning, the ways you're growing—none of those are just for you. As soon as you can, start passing on what God has entrusted to you.

The legacy of a believer is not limited to the physical children we have, but rather much of it is found in the spiritual children we raise up and release into the kingdom.

Your God-sized dream is made to outlive you. It will look different in each generation, but the heart of it will remain the same. Only God can see how your piece of a God-sized dream fits into his overall plan for all of history.

Your God-sized dream is eternal. So make the most of it today. And then pass it on for tomorrow.

Explore

Read Psalm 33 for more glimpses into God's eternal plan.

Express

God, you have no beginning and no end. While I'm limited by time, you are eternal. That's hard for me to even grasp. I thank you for letting me be part of what you're doing in this generation through my God-sized dream. Show me how to be a wise steward of what you've entrusted me with now and how I can pass it on to others as well. Amen.

Opening the Door to Your God-Sized Dream

Experience

Draw the "family tree" of your God-sized dream. Who has influenced you? And who can you pass your God-sized dream to in the future?

When It's Time to Pass Your Dream On to Someone New

39

Yes, You're Allowed to Be Happy

The LORD be exalted,
  who delights in the well-being of
    his servant.

                              Psalm 35:27

Our story begins with a God-sized dream. Adam and Eve live in Eden, in the perfect place God created for them. Our world, our very existence, is a dream come true for God.

Then sin enters the picture, and the God-sized dream is broken. But God doesn't give up. He chooses a people as his own and delivers them from slavery. The desire of his heart is to lead them into a Promised Land.

But the people rebel and once again God redirects. He lets them wander in the desert before they can enter what he has for them. Then they rebel again and are exiled from the place where they belong.

But God still doesn't give up. He sends a Savior to redeem us—a way for us to enter the ultimate Promised Land that he's preparing for us. It's Eden for eternity.

When we look at what God wants for us, it's clear we're made to dwell in joy. Yes, Scripture talks about suffering too. But that is always temporary. Even in the most famous story of all concerning suffering, when Job loses everything, God restores it to him (and then some) in the end.

Somehow modern Christianity seems to have gotten a bit confused about that somewhere along the way. We can see the desert of suffering as a place we're supposed to live in—not as a place we are only passing through on the way to what God has for us. And the Promised Land isn't only heaven. (I talk extensively about how

Scripture shows that to be true in *You're Going to Be Okay*.)

What you need to know now as you pursue your God-sized dream is that you can and should fight for joy. If you're a dreamer in today's world you're likely to be told, "You're too positive" or "You need to live in reality." Joy and happiness are not popular, in spite of how much we may say we want them.

Yet they are what God desires for us. In *The Law of Happiness*, Henry Cloud explains: "One of my favorite words that we hear over and over in the Bible is the Hebrew word shalom, which among other things implies peace, happiness, well-being, wholeness, completeness, and welfare—most of what we mean when we say we want to be 'happy.'"[1]

Cloud goes on to share how research shows that circumstances only make up about ten percent of our happiness. Genetics plays a role too. But we can significantly influence our overall well-being by choosing to live God's way. He concludes, "That leaves us all with a decision. Or better yet, an entire lifetime of decisions. Moment by moment, day by day, year by year, decade by decade, choices create a direction. . . . We all have the choice to invest ourselves in living in ways that produce happiness."[2]

If you're reading this book, then you're already making the kind of choices that lead to Promised Land living. You are saying yes to whatever God has for you. You're moving forward in faith. You're persevering and being a woman of courage.

The world will oppose you when you live this way—it will try to drag you back to the desert or tell you you're a fool. So lean in and listen to this: "Keep choosing joy. Keep dreaming. Keep believing what God says . . . no matter what."

Dare to believe you're not only allowed to live in joy, but you're actually called to do so. It's a scandalous truth that will set you apart and set you up to receive God's best for you.

Explore

Read the description of the Promised Land in Deuteronomy 8.

Express

God, I'm so glad that you "delight in the well-being of your servant." You told us that we will have trouble in this world but that through you we can overcome it. Your desire is for us to thrive and to live with joy. Help me to embrace that truth in my life and share it with others. Amen.

Experience

What lies have you been believing about joy and happiness? Write them down and replace them with the truth of what God desires for you instead.

Opening the Door to Your God-Sized Dream

40

The One Thing
You Must Not Do

*In all these things we are more than
conquerors through him who loved us.*

Romans 8:37

We've talked about it before but it's worth saying
again as we reach the end of this journey: *God
loves messy people.*

The wild ones.
The kind we might pass by.
David—the murderer and adulterer.

Peter—the fisherman with rough edges.

Rahab—the lady of the night who found the light.

It doesn't make any sense to us. We would pick the ones who have it all together. The ones who didn't cause such a scene. The ones who played by the rules.

So what do the people God chooses have in common?

They don't quit.

The mistakes they make are astounding.

The baggage they carry could fill a huge truck.

The stunts they pull would get most of us fired.

But they never stop.

They fall down and get back up.

They say the wrong thing and then repent.

They fail and stubbornly press forward anyway.

That is the one thing you must not do on the way to your God-sized dream: you must not quit. When you really get down to it, that's all God requires.

And not quitting doesn't mean not giving up on your dream. Sometimes you will realize you have been chasing entirely the wrong one and the wisest thing you can do is stop. What I mean is that *you never quit pursuing Jesus.*

> You never quit saying yes when he asks you to do something crazy.
>
> You never quit letting him teach you through your mistakes.
>
> You never quit giving it one more try, even when you're scared silly.

That is what brings God joy, my friend. Not when you're "perfect" on the outside. Not when you have a tidy existence. Not when you get it right the first time.

Nope, God loves it when you will stop at nothing to have more of him in your life. That's really what God-sized dreams are all about anyway. I hope you know that by now—that our dreams are really just ways that we chase the One who has been pursuing our hearts even before we were born.

The ultimate goal is not an outcome. It's an outpouring of more of Jesus in our lives. It's

The One Thing You Must Not Do

experiencing intimacy with him in ways we never have before. It's learning, growing, and letting him transform us from the inside out.

Just this morning I got up to write and an email caught me off guard. Before I knew it, instead of having lofty thoughts to put on the page, I was fighting the urge to think unprintable words. And then the accusations kicked in: "Who are you to even talk about this when you're such a mess?" Ever heard that too? I imagine you have—we all do. But the answer is that God has never been afraid to use messy people.

So I said, "God, I need a do-over. Forgive me and help me start again." Then I sat down at the keyboard one more time.

That's what we're all to do. God has taken care of your sins, failures, and mistakes on the cross. Those aren't the biggest obstacle in your God-sized dream anymore. What's far more dangerous is letting those things convince you that you should quit because you'll never be worthy.

Don't listen to that lie. Not today. Not ever.

You're not a quitter.

You're more than a conqueror.

You're also a God-sized dreamer.

Messy, beautiful, broken, and whole.

The only kind God uses.

And he's going to use you beyond what you can even imagine.

Explore

Read Romans 8:31–39 to see how nothing can get between you and God's love.

Express

God, it's so freeing to know I don't need to "have it all together" to be used by you. Thank you for taking care of my sinfulness and brokenness through Christ's death on the cross. I receive what you have done for me and I offer up all I have, all I am to you today. And I choose to

be a God-sized dreamer for the rest of my life!
Amen.

Experience

You've spent forty days pursuing your God-sized dreams, and yet you've only just begun. What's your next step? Take some time to think and pray about it. Then go do it, girl. The best is yet to be for you!

Acknowledgments

This book is a God-sized dream come true for me.

As always, thanks to my fabulous team at Revell for all you do. You're more than my publisher. You're partners and friends. I'm especially grateful for my editorial and marketing girls—Jennifer Leep, Wendy Wetzel, Michele Misiak, Robin Barnett, and Twila Bennett.

Thanks to my strong and wise husband, Mark, who has his feet on the ground so I can keep my head in the clouds and my fingers on the keyboard. I love you.

To the God-sized dream girls in my real life and online, you are a gift, and I wouldn't be able to do this without you. Thank you for cheering me on and for being women of courage who teach me new things every day.

Most of all, to the Giver of dreams—thank you for letting me write with and for you. I'm your servant; may it be to me as you have said. Use me as little or as much as you want. And may my life bring you great joy.

Notes

Chapter 4: The Secret No One Tells You

1. Keri Lynn, "The Dream Giver," *Holley Gerth* (blog), May 7, 2013, http://holleygerth.com/god-sized-dreams-guest-post-keri-lynn.

Chapter 5: The Backstory to Your God-Sized Dream

1. Melanie Self, comment on Holley Gerth, "God-Sized Dreams: The Backstory (and a Few Confessions)," January 4, 2013, http://holleygerth.com/god-sized-dreams-the-backstory-and-a-few-confessions/#comments.

Chapter 13: You're Never a Failure

1. Jim Elliot, Billy Graham Center Archives, Wheaton College, updated May 31, 2012, http://www2.wheaton.edu/bgc/archives/faq/20.htm.

Chapter 19: When Your God-Sized Dream Gets Hard

1. Henry Cloud and John Townsend, *How People Grow: What the Bible Reveals about Personal Growth* (Grand Rapids: Zondervan, 2009), 82.

2. Ibid.

Chapter 20: When You Want to Compare

1. Jon Acuff, "Avoiding One Great Temptation Every New Dream Faces," guest post on *MichaelHyatt.com* (blog), May 11, 2011, http://michaelhyatt.com/avoiding-one-great-temptation-every-new-dream-faces.html.

Chapter 29: Be Who You Want to Be Around

1. Daniel Goleman, *Social Intelligence: The New Science of Human Relationships* (New York: Bantam Dell, 2007), 60.

Chapter 32: When You Really Want to Change the World

1. Genny Heika, "My God-Sized Dream," *Genny Heika* (blog), January 7, 2013, http://gennyheikka.com/2013/01/the-backstory-to-my-god-sized-dream.html.

2. Ibid.

Chapter 33: What Every God-Sized Dream Ultimately Points Our Hearts To

1. Jennifer Camp, "When I Speak Aloud My God-Sized Dream," *You Are My Girls* (blog), January 8, 2013, http://

www.youaremygirls.com/2013/01/08/when-i-speak
-aloud-my-god-sized-dream/.

Chapter 34: What If Someone Else Is Already Living Your Dream?

1. Lisa-Jo Baker, "Why You Don't Have to Be Afraid That Someone Will Steal Your Dream," *The Gypsy Mama* (blog), August 23, 2012, http://lisajobaker.com/2012/08/ why-dont-afraid-someone-will-steal-dream/.

Chapter 36: When Your Heart Needs Some Encouragement

1. Michele-Lyn Ault, "STAND (Dream Again Day 8)," *A Life Surrendered* (blog), January 8, 2013, http://www.alife surrendered.com/2013/01/stand-dream-again-bonus-day/.

Chapter 39: Yes, You're Allowed to Be Happy

1. Henry Cloud, *The Law of Happiness* (New York: Howard Books, 2011), Kindle Edition, 77.

2. Ibid.

About Holley

Holley Gerth is a bestselling writer, speaker, and life coach who loves sharing God's heart with women through words. She's done so through several books, a partnership with DaySpring, and her popular blog. Holley is also a cofounder of (in)courage, a website for women that received almost a million page views in its first six months. Holley now does e-coaching for God-sized dreamers, and you can find out more at www.holleygerth.com.

Holley shares her heart and home with her husband, Mark. She lives in the South, likes to say "y'all," and would love to have coffee with you so she could hear all about you too. Until then, she hopes you'll hang out with her online at www.holleygerth.com.

Hello, friend!

Thanks again for sharing this journey with me. I truly wish I could have a cup of coffee with you today and hear about your God-sized dreams. Until then, I hope we can stay connected in some other ways!

This devotional is intended to be a companion to the book, *You're Made for a God-Sized Dream: Opening the Door to All God Has for You*. That book will give you even more encouragement and tools as you pursue your God-sized dreams. It's also a great resource for groups.

I'd love for you to stop by my place online, **www.holleygerth.com**, for more encouragement too. The e-coaching section will tell you about one way I can partner with you in your God-sized dream. And when you subscribe by email to the blog, you'll get free messages from me sent right to your inbox.

With Jesus you really are made for more, my friend. Keep believing that's true and dreaming like you do!

Love,

Holley Gerth

PS: Together we can help women all over the world fulfill their God-sized dreams. A portion of author proceeds from this book will go to the Compassion International Leadership Development Program. To find out more about the program, visit **www.compassion.com**.

Discover the dreams God has given you—
and then dare to pursue them.

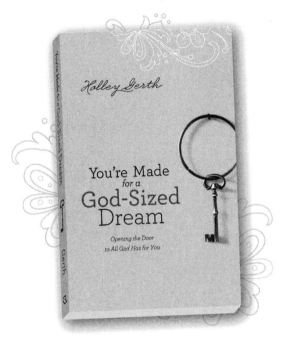

Holley Gerth takes you by the heart and says,
"Yes! You can do this!" She guides you with insightful
questions, action plans to take the next steps, and
most of all, the loving hand of a friend.

ℛ Revell
a division of Baker Publishing Group
www.RevellBooks.com

This ebook is the perfect companion to
Holley's *You're Made for a God-Sized Dream*.

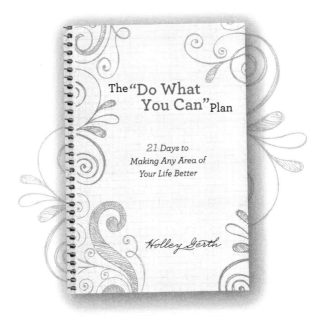

No matter what change you'd like to see in your life, you can make
progress in just three weeks by taking new steps and overcoming the
obstacles that have been getting in your way. Bestselling author and life
coach Holley Gerth will be your partner on this journey. Her 21-day
"Do What You Can" Plan guides you closer to God's best for you through
encouraging Scriptures, personal stories, and practical action tools.

 Revell
a division of Baker Publishing Group
www.RevellBooks.com

Available in Ebook Format

"Holley Gerth turns words like a poet. Warm and personal, *You're Already Amazing* is a biblical, practical handbook for every woman's heart."

— Emily P. Freeman, author of *Grace for the Good Girl*

With this heart-to-heart message, Holley Gerth invites you to embrace one very important truth—that you truly are already amazing. Like a trusted friend, Holley gently shows you how to forget the lies and expectations the world feeds you and instead believe that God loves you and has bigger plans for your life than you've even imagined.

Ⱅ Revell
a division of Baker Publishing Group
www.RevellBooks.com